D1232630

Forgetting The Memories:
A Caregiver's Journey Through Alzheimer's Disease

ROY D. STEINBERG, PH.D.

authorHOUSE®

AuthorHouse™
1663 Liberty Drive
Bloomington, IN 47403
www.authorhouse.com
Phone: 1-800-839-8640

First published by AuthorHouse 1/11/2010

ISBN: 978-1-4490-5590-5 (e)
ISBN: 978-1-4490-5588-2 (sc)
ISBN: 978-1-4490-5589-9 (hc)

Library of Congress Control Number: 2009912791

Printed in the United States of America
Bloomington, Indiana

This book is printed on acid-free paper.

Author's Note

Personal experiences can, at times, help professionals more meaningfully relate to the concerns of their clients. Revealing these experiences is not without its risks. My family's situation, as related to Alzheimer's disease, is directly in my area of expertise, which allowed me a greater opportunity to share my understanding and resources.

Writing this book has exposed me to the potential risk of family resentment or even hostility. It may also suggest the appearance of being too close to a situation to allow for objectivity. On the other hand, such an intimate journey may provide a more in depth vantage point into certain realities of life.

My training has prepared me to understand and counsel regarding aspects of Alzheimer's disease and other dementias. This is easier said than done when Alzheimer's disease hits home, confronting personal and emotional issues. However, such a personal experience adds an additional perspective and multi-layered understanding of the thoughts and feelings confronting caregivers.

I have tried not to hold back in revealing my personal concerns, thoughts, and reactions because I believe the history and progression of my mother's experience demonstrates one of the more difficult examples of denial, and the frustrations and difficulties in trying to "do the right thing."

My hope is to be objective in my descriptions, but the subjective cannot be hidden. Even professionals may be too close at times. My effort in this book is to balance the risks with the rewards to create a platform for understanding the intricacies and dynamics that are intertwined in the experiences of Alzheimer's disease, for the loved one and for the caregiver, without jeopardizing my family's integrity.

CHAPTER 1.

My Mother...and Alzheimer's disease

For my mother, music was always more than a pastime. It was a passion. Although she'd never played professionally, she studied piano as a child, and music – classical, the symphony – was a significant part of her life from early on. I can still remember going to the symphony with her, both as a child in Israel and later, when my family immigrated to New York City. Long before I understood what she was doing, how she was building in me the same appreciation she had, I can recall her asking me questions, getting me to talk about the music to which we were listening.

My mother is a diminutive woman, not much over five feet. As a young adult, she was extremely thin, almost emaciated at times. She has short blond hair, which has varied with the style of the times. I have pictures of her when she was in her twenties. She was a gentle-looking woman, pretty in her own way. She dressed casually, but certainly had the ability to dress up for an occasion. My father always bought her the best jewels, but she never wore too much or appeared pretentious.

Her voice, to me, sounds harsh. Not coarse, exactly, but not gentle or mellifluous either. Despite this, she loves to sing. She has always been very musical, and long enjoyed the classics and swing. No matter what I think of her singing, it is from her that I gained my love for music. I always joke that I was born in the wrong era, because I enjoy classical and swing just as much as contemporary and even rock music.

When she was younger, my mother was also a wonderful dancer. At one of my parents' anniversaries, we dined at the St. Regis Hotel, where my father was the chief engineer. After dinner, the musicians played as my parents danced. I vividly remember watching my mother twirling around my father, who was the consummate dance partner, moving with minimal effort, but exuding style. I don't suppose it's a stretch to suggest that my love for ballroom dancing comes from watching them move across the floor with such grace and finesse.

What does this mean, now, when so much of my mother is gone? I'm not sure. But I do know that reflection is healthy medicine. A reminder of what she was like when she was whole. My mother is now 76, truly a shadow of her former self. In my professional role as a geriatric psychologist, I know where she is heading. But that didn't make it easier to spot the first signs of decline. It never is, although we as the family members are usually the first to notice when something has changed, when something has "gone wrong." For me, that pivotal moment came about eight years ago – but I now suspect that the change may have begun some time before. Looking back at those days, I can see why it was so hard to spot the first signs, the first symptoms of her illness.

Music meant so much to my mother. Even before we moved to New York, in 1974, she would take us to hear the Israeli Philharmonic. "Us" being my brother and me. My father, now 75, was never interested in such artsy pursuits, and as such, it was something that my mother got to enjoy only with her sons or her sister, my Aunt Ruhama, whose own husband, my Uncle Zelig, was much more amenable to, or at least tolerant of, cultural pursuits.

For us, these evenings were fancy affairs. In Israel, at least in those days, people did not dress up particularly formally. Still, on such special occasions, the women wore dresses and the men donned jackets, which all seemed in keeping with the glamorous hall, the grand staircases, and the bright chandeliers. You could just imagine a princess walking down the winding staircase to greet the commoners, searching for her prince on such a special occasion. Or at least that's how it felt to me, then nine years old. I don't recall what we heard, or even what I thought of the music – other than that I was supposed to appear interested. I sat there, looking intent and intense, all the while waiting for intermission, my favorite part, because that was when I'd get a snack. Back then, by now over thirty years ago, a soda and a chocolate bar seemed like the best of the best. My favorite chocolate bar had small nougats, I recall, somewhat similar to the more common Snickers bar of today. Back then, though, it seemed so much more special and unique.

As I enjoyed my treat, I remember my mother asking me about the music. Which piece was my favorite? Why? Guiding me in terms of visualizing what the music was trying to communicate. Back then I couldn't fathom what she was doing, despite her constant attentions. I simply wanted to enjoy my chocolate. My brother might have had a greater appreciation; he became a classical pianist and in many ways, my mother lived through him. She went to all his concert performances and competitions, telling anyone who would listen that if he didn't win it was because the judging was "fixed." At times, this may have not been the most productive outlook for her – or for my brother, who was raised with her, at times, unhealthy certainty that any apparently negative outcome was the doing of others.

But although a passion for and about music was something my mother could share with her two sons, it wasn't something she could bring her husband, my father, into. My father is truly a "man's man." As a young man he stood six feet tall, with a beautiful wave of dark hair. In pictures of him, he is standing next to a classic Cadillac, which he owned when he was young, the true image of "cool." He had a clear view of what a man should be, what real men did, and there was no diverting him, for better or worse. He was, and is, strictly a "sports and news guy." The arts were my mother's territory. Not that he lacked discernment. An electrical engineer, he also built clocks – beautiful pieces – for his own pleasure, and later on showed his own fine aesthetics when he began working in stained glass. I still proudly display a piece he gave me on the occasion of my first marriage. A beautiful Tiffany-style lamp shade, with small green "leaves" drooping down. Its beauty and quality lie not in its size, but in its excruciatingly fine details, a skill for any craftsman. These were his pursuits, and while he used them generously to make gifts, he was not interested in sharing his wife's consuming passion.

Maybe that's why the initial disconnect about my mother's disease, her cognitive decline, was so difficult for him to see and understand. After all, she was the artistic one, the one who valued something he couldn't see and wouldn't hear. Men and women were different. She was always "emotional," always touchy about things that mattered to her and that he didn't, and never would, understand. That's just the way things were.

My mother's cognitive decline first manifested itself more directly at work. If you knew my mother, this would make sense: Office life was never simple for my mother, at least for as long as I knew her. She graduated law school in Israel and worked as a lawyer, focusing on family law, in the office of a general practitioner. After my family immigrated to New York City, she was never able to get her career up and running to her satisfaction again. Instead, unable to get licensed in this country, she worked as a travel agent, putting her worldly experience abroad and her command of languages to use.

The step down – in income, in status – rankled her soul in the harshest of ways. In Israel, she was a star, a charming woman, a professional, truly a bon vivant. That began to change once we moved to New York. She had no true friends to speak of, though others worked hard to befriend her. Instead of being a highly trained professional, she was a travel agent – an employee. And she was not happy working for others. She worked for one company for about a decade, and then was forced out, told that Israelis could only work for a specific period of time so as not to encourage emigration out of Israel. I never knew if this was truly a company policy or simply a way to get rid of "troublemakers." But it didn't matter. She got another job, with a different agency, but that one only lasted for a short while. Finally, she ended up at a small agency, a start-up headed by a woman who was a client of hers at her previous agency. Evelyn, the owner, worked hard to befriend my mother, and I've always suspected that she gave my mother the job primarily out of her sense of friendship. Evelyn was more reflective of my mother's style. A delicate woman, she stood tall though never towering. She was graceful in her presence and spoke gently and with refinement.

Not that my mother wasn't a smart, competent woman in those days. She truly was. Educated in all aspects, she could quote literature and the Bible, appreciate Monet and Chagall, and sing and dance to Frank Sinatra. But she had an attitude, and this has long been her limitation. Everyone else was always in the wrong, and because of their errors – their shortsightedness – she was always the victim. Maybe, in retrospect, back when she was working for Evelyn, she was also beginning to show the first signs of Alzheimer's. Maybe she felt her grasp slipping, saw errors appear in her own work, and lashed out defensively in reaction to her own fear. I will never know.

What I do know, however, suggests that Alzheimer's disease had likely already begun, almost imperceptibly, to strip her of her capabilities by the time of this last job. By the time she went to work for Evelyn, she was already making significant mistakes. Incorrect bookings, schedules that didn't accommodate all the activities of a tour, not arranging for tickets to be ready in time for a tour. All simple things, really, but seriously disruptive to the business – and to my mother's sense of self.

Whatever the reason for these errors, she reacted by striking out. Her personality has always been such that she blamed others for failures, and it became easy for her to take this approach here. "Nobody likes me. They're all out to get me." She'd come home and talk with my father about this, venting her frustration and resentment.

"Nothing ever goes my way," she'd say, threatening, once again, for the millionth time, or so it felt, to quit. "Nothing ever goes my way." My father would sit and listen, one eye on the news, or the Yankees, the Rangers or whatever sporting event was on at that time, responding when the tirade died down with robot-like predictability.

"What do you want me to tell you?" he would ask, his eyes still on the game. "If you want to quit, quit!"

My mother's income was never a substantial part of the family finances, and so he didn't consider it in making any decisions. For him, the burden of listening to her was not worth the money she was making. And as time went on, her complaints increased in frequency and intensity. Nothing was ever her fault, even when the errors began to pile up. She was always blaming the boss, even when that boss was her friend Evelyn, or a client.

I sympathized, and at least at first wondered why my father didn't seem to care. She was my mother, and, at least back then, I had a different, more palpable affection for her. Like my father, I had heard these same complaints for many years when I lived at home and after, when I'd visit or call. They had become part and parcel of my image of my mother. When I was younger, I never questioned her veracity. Why would I? To a child, the world did seem daunting – and my mother, like any mother, was my savior. If she said that others were at fault, I had no reason to doubt her. As I grew up, I just accepted this side of her: put upon, complaining, the perfectionist suffering through the imperfect world.

But something else was at work. Something besides her usual sensitive nature, and as I advanced in my professional career I began to see things in a new way. I remember what I believe was my first perception of a warning signal, a possible first sign of her decline. I had stopped by her office one day, simply for the pleasure of watching her work. As a young man. I truly enjoyed visiting my parents at work. It gave me a sense of connection. But what I saw was not comforting in any sense. What I saw was my mother scrambling around for numbers, clearly at a loss. Not searching the way that a business woman does, with determination, set upon righting a clumsy wrong or locating a temporarily mislaid file. But casting about in an out-of-control manner, with the frenetic energy of a person who simply cannot fathom that she would make a mistake, and assumes that if only she searches hard enough she will find the missing number.

It's possible that she might have known too, maybe on some level, that something else was going on. Not only did her level of complaining – the sound of desperation – begin to ratchet up, but she also, belatedly, began studying for the New York Bar exam. She would be a lawyer again. She would be done with stupid bosses, with annoying clients, with silly mistakes. She'd be in control again – of her career, her life. Her mind. Such plans are fairly common with the early stages of dementia.

People can feel unrealistically confident, genuinely believing they can fully and independently manage their own lives. After all, they always have. But they may also feel the life they knew slipping away, and may strike out, trying to regain control.

Therefore, before Evelyn, but thirty years after she had anything to do with the law – and in another country, to boot – she decided to study for the New York bar exam. And she believed, or at least seemed to believe, with all her heart, that through study and the sheer force of will she would pass the strenuous exam and get her license. She must have realized she was failing, but she would make this come to be through pure will power and hard work. Such was the strength of her conviction, which, at the time, I believed was part of her inner strength. Later, I would come to see it as also a part of her disease.

My mother studied hard, every night, buying books and study aids. Like a youngster fresh out of law school, she signed up and completed the Kaplan prep course. When I came to visit on the weekends, I observed what she was doing, since she'd converted my old room into her study area, filling it with books and sample tests. That room, which had once seemed spacious, seemed to shrink with age as it filled with her study materials, and with her desperation.

My mother was trying. Trying to bring back a sense of competence. My old desk was piled with her books, and I knew she spent hours in there, studying and memorizing the codes and formalities of her adopted country. She fared remarkably well – dare I use such a pejorative term? – passing the multiple choice portion, but not the written portion of this long, intense, and difficult exam. This is no small feat for anyone, let alone a woman in her late sixties. During this time my mother was able to get a job as a paralegal, working for a general practitioner. Her resumé reflects a woman highly qualified, undaunted by age or disease. She drafted documents, filed papers with the court. What the resume fails to mention, as my father has since recalled to me, were her frustrations when she could not fully prepare a document to her boss's liking, and the ensuing feelings of anger, always aimed at others.

I do remember her talking about her frustrations with that job, her desire to once again be a lawyer. To have a profession. I would nod knowingly, the sadness always within me, one I could not find a way to express. She always felt that life had passed her by. She wanted to be respected by those around her. It wasn't fair that she wasn't – and it wasn't her fault, either.

When she would get into this groove, I would gently, and sometimes not so subtly, try to move the conversation onto other topics. Should I have realized that something was happening sooner? Perhaps. After all, I am not only a family member, but also a professional who specializes in this field. But work was the one area where my mother was independent of the family. For many people who struggle with the early stages of Alzheimer's there are many potential indicators for the onset of the disease. Everyday tasks are neglected or done poorly. Normal activities start to slip. But in our family, finances, driving, yes, even cooking – all the other areas where first signs are sometimes noted in other families – were handled by my father. And he wasn't seeing anything.

Then again, why should he? To my father, my mother was just being herself – only a little more so. At home, she had virtually no responsibilities, so there were no mishaps for him to witness. He didn't work with her, so he didn't see the mistakes she made there. He only heard the complaining, which was not in any way unusual for her. She was, he would tell me, "trying to make my life miserable."

"What's new?" I would ask every time I'd call.

"What do you want me to tell you?" he would invariably respond, with what would become a characteristically heavy sigh. "Your mother drives me crazy, but that's just the way she is."

Even as her cognitive decline became more apparent, he attributed her behaviors to her personality style. Neither of them was willing to – nor knew how to – face the reality: My mother was losing her memory; they had to make plans to deal with it. But they didn't want to. They didn't want to face the future, in any form. Maybe it wasn't so much that they didn't want to. Rather, they weren't able.

I vividly remember (an ironic turn of phrase given the topic of my book), some time ago, when I visited my parents in New York and we all sat around the dining table. The apartment was in a "pre-war" building. It was considered relatively large, the housing market in New York being what it is. It was entered through a small entrance hall, where you would find two closets facing you, and one to your left. This entrance way immediately transitioned into the dining area, not "formal," but one that would serve as such, adjoining the kitchen. My father had "picked up" an antique table, a western-style table. It had carved-in grooves on two sides - he told us this was designed years ago to place tips after a meal. The "chandelier" was a wagon wheel design with spokes. I never thought much of this style, but once having left home, when I came back it began to stand out more and more, a symbol of time passed, and passing. My parents never changed the furniture, until they finally moved from New York. Did I mention that change was never easy for my parents, not even in these little things? And if they couldn't deal with furniture, how would they face bigger shifts in health and expectations?

During that visit, we were supposed to be talking about financial planning. That is, they said they would be willing to talk about money, for once, and I was trying to stress the need for some forward planning. Well, they might have said they were willing to discuss planning, but in reality it was rough sledding. My father is old school. Whenever I brought up an idea, a program for estate planning, he dismissed me off-handedly, saying, "I'm not planning on dying any time soon."

I could feel myself getting frustrated at this willful blindness. I tried to keep my voice calm as I explained the issues about aging, particularly as they related to memory loss. I tried to be strategic. I didn't single out my mother: I explained to both of them how prevalent a concern memory loss was across the United States, and what problems it could bring. Both of them summarily dismissed my concerns. To quote my mother: "When I go crazy you can have all my money."

I don't know why this bothered me. I knew from my work that this reaction was quite common. The association of "craziness" and Alzheimer's has long been prevalent, particularly among the older people most at risk. Even today, a number of years later, when I evaluate older adults, they often, and quite matter of fact, ask me, "are you trying to see if I'm crazy?" The confusion probably comes from the word "dementia," which has a strong negative connotation, dating back to the 1960's and possibly earlier, when institutionalized individuals were deemed to be "demented" or crazy.

I tried again in more recent years. My parents had joined my wife and me for dinner, and somehow the conversation came around to the topic of estate planning. My mother was resisting making some changes, now becoming suspicious that I would steal her money, even though there is very little to "steal". Once again, I felt my temper flare.

At some point during the conversation my mother bluntly asked whether I thought she was "losing it." Credit my frustration; at the time I was lacking the professional distance I have since embraced when interacting with her. I found myself mercilessly blurting, "Yes, you are! You have a significant memory problem and you need to acknowledge it."

The pain was insufferable, not just for her, but for me. I knew I had overstepped the boundaries of healthy self expression, but I couldn't help myself. I was frustrated by her reticence, by her complete unwillingness – inability? – even to consider what I had been trying to present. Even my best desire – to help – played against us both as it was quickly overwhelmed by a stronger impulse to "fix it all" in one fell swoop. This isn't only a professional's problem. Many family members, I know, fall prey to these same desires when first confronted by the disease. Although I would subsequently recognize my dual role as a professional and caregiving family member, and learn to control my desire to speak before thinking, I know at that moment I was acting, at least partly, like an overwhelmed family member: frustrated, angry, and maybe even somewhat weighed down.

My outburst had the opposite reaction than what I wanted. My mother quickly became sullen and stopped talking. My father switched the topic, and my wife, with a more gentle touch, tried to bring us all back to the issue of estate planning. By then, my mother would have none of it. Nor would she discuss it the next day. But not, I discovered, because she was still angry. Instead, she had forgotten the conversation completely, and my father was content to let it go. To him, the easiest way to deal with her disease was, and remains, avoidance. He's a practical man, living in the here and now, and his concerns are pragmatic ones: How she was coping. Whether she would talk to him that day or not. He doesn't let himself worry about her decline. He doesn't let himself think about her memory, or how much of it she has already lost. He doesn't let himself think about the future. In a way, his everyday coping skills have made it easy for him to slide into what can only be termed denial.

I've since tried to talk to my father many times about my mother's memory loss. Tried to break through the denial before the reality gets so bad that even he cannot maintain the illusion of normalcy. We speak almost every day. We meet for Friday night dinner, lunch every other week with the kids, and occasionally dine during the week with him and my wife. My mother often refuses to attend, complaining she is sick. The ailment is irrelevant, as mostly this is just somatization, a sense of being sick, rather than any actual malady. I've almost stopped asking about her well-being, usually because the responses are mostly vague and only perpetuate the negative. My kids often ask, "Is Safta (grandmother) coming?" Most of the time they answer themselves: "Oh no, she's probably sick." We care, painfully so. But we have all become somewhat desensitized.

It is during these meals that I try to engage my father in a more significant discussion, trying to walk him through the specifics of her memory loss. I try to help him make the distinction between her memory loss and her personality quirks. I explain that, "in the past when Ema (mom) became sullen or withdrawn, that may have been more of her character, her personal struggle to consider alternatives. Now, when she withdraws, it is more related to her cognitive difficulty, maybe we should even say inability, in considering alternatives. At times it's a heavy burden, almost literally, on her brain to think."

I often try to draw a parallel for him: "Imagine what it would be like for you, as an engineer, to be confronted with blueprints, and not be able to understand them, despite knowing that in the past you were fully competent in this area. Ema's withdrawal is now more about what has become of her, rather than who she was."

I encourage him to let go of the "image" of her in the past, and begin to view her realistically. But he is not ready. Like any old "habit," change comes slowly, and with great reluctance.

Maybe it was easier for me. After all, my mother's problems were already familiar to me because of my work. By the time I was noticing my mother's memory loss, at the turn of the millennium, I had finished graduate school, had completed a well regarded post-doctoral fellowship at the Philadelphia Geriatric Center, worked for a couple of years at Presbyterian Hospital in Philadelphia in the older adult Partial Day Hospital Program, and had ventured out into private practice, working in nursing homes and assisted living settings. Although I was not as knowledgeable as I believe myself to be today, I had developed sufficient understanding of her condition to recognize there was a decline, that it was not "normal aging," and I knew the signs to look for. The problem was that she was still fairly high functioning and intelligent at that time. Therefore, those who did not have my education, my experience in working with older adults, and my awareness of my mother's "baseline functioning" – her level of education and her professional success – would view as normal what my professional eye recognized as early indications of cognitive decline.

I am learning to accept that others are not as readily aware of her difficulties.

A few years ago we were scheduled to have a birthday celebration for my mother. I made reservations for a special brunch at a nearby catering hall. Fancy, striving, but never quite living up to its effort at appearing to be of "five star" caliber – but still a big deal, with musicians, lovely floral decorations, and beautiful, serene water fountains welcoming visitors outside the entrance. The kind of place my mother, who embraces all that is fancy, would usually love. Only, this time she decided at the last minute that she wouldn't go. I don't know why, but I do know that people with memory loss sometimes act in a contrary manner. Maybe she had forgotten about it and thought the invitation was some kind of a trick. Maybe she was confused, and by refusing to budge she felt like she was regaining some kind of control. Maybe, with the knowledge of her decline in the back of her mind, she simply rejected the idea of celebrating another birthday. Whatever her reasoning, she created the kind of predicament that now has become common.

"Never, never again," my father said when he called to tell me the news, frustrated and angry by what he saw as her ridiculous whim. "Never!" Such absolutes no longer make sense in our brave new world. With some effort, I was able to calm my father down. Though outside my comfort zone, I've learned to work with the situation, and so, with a bit of a contrived cough, I called the catering hall and was able to change the reservation, and move the $100 deposit, to a month later. Predictably, by the next day, my mother had forgotten the entire affair. We went to brunch a month later, which coincided with Valentine's Day, and this time my mother was genuinely excited.

I call my father daily, just to check in and to see if he needs anything. In part, I want to give him an opportunity to let off steam.

"Ma nishmah?" I ask him in Hebrew. "What's new?"

I always hear the now familiar sigh, but I have to follow up. "Ma yesh?" "What's happening? Is something wrong?"

The same thing, it's always the same thing. "She's not talking to me."

"She is *not* 'not talking' to you." For the fiftieth or hundredth time, I try to explain. "She is sick. This is just how she is."

Another sigh, longer and more pronounced. "Yeah, yeah," he says, before summarily concluding "I'll talk to you later" and hanging up. He's not mad at me, just mad at his lot in life. He cannot bring himself to see that his wife just isn't his wife anymore.

CHAPTER 2.

The Difference Between "Normal" Forgetfulness and True Memory Deficits

When we talk about memory loss, it helps to have a basic understanding of how aging affects our brains. Although we think of memory loss as something that happens when we are "old," say in our sixties or older, it really begins much earlier. Every individual is different, of course, but generally speaking, cognition begins to decline in most people in our early thirties, so to say that forgetting is normal as we age is almost a given. The question we really should be asking is whether the forgetting, or cognitive decline, is within or outside the expected or normal range of decline.

What about those familiar so-called "senior moments"? The idea that older people are more prone to forgetting is largely an aspect of ageism. In fact, people who are having such a senior moment are just as likely having what may more accurately be termed an "inattentive moment." They are distracted by various events, which make it difficult to retrieve information. If left alone, and given time to "clear their heads," the "forgotten" information is often retrieved. Such an occurrence is what we all recognize as the "tip of the tongue" phenomenon; we know the answer or the word or the name, we just need a moment of peace in which to retrieve it. It is only when such so-called "senior moments" are persistent and the person cannot retrieve the information, even when there are no internal or external stressors, that we should consider that there may be a more pervasive and structural underlying problem, one that requires a different type of professional assessment and intervention.

What those underlying problems may be can vary greatly. Before we start labeling someone as having Alzheimer's disease, or any other form of dementia, we need to rule out many other possibilities. For example, there may be other medical conditions that can affect how we think, and how we remember, but which may be temporary and treatable. Urinary tract infections, for example, may affect older people much more significantly than younger people, and an older woman with a common UTI may seem quite "out of it," and not herself. Depression may also mimic some of the symptoms, as may the side effects of various medications. Since these are generally treatable conditions, cognitive impairment or memory loss associated with them would be considered transient, temporary, and not necessarily a sign of Alzheimer's disease.

What professionals need to do is establish a baseline. In other words, find out what is normal for that person. After any temporary condition has been ruled out or treated, then the clinician can begin to see what that person's baseline of functioning is – and compare it to how that person used to be. In other words, if someone wasn't a rocket scientist before the suspected decline, it would be unfair to ask him to master Euclidian Geometry now. However, if the person had been highly functioning and well educated, as, for example, my mother was, her baseline is expected to be fairly high. If the person consistently does not meet what has been his or her baseline and there isn't a treatable, temporary medical, psychological, or other evident cause, then we have to consider the possibility of some form of dementia, such as Alzheimer's.

Although we tend to use the word Alzheimer's as a catch-all, there are numerous types of dementia. Statistically, if a person is diagnosed with any form of dementia, the odds of that dementia being what is clinically known as SDAT, or senile dementia of the Alzheimer's Type (colloquially Alzheimer's), is 60 - 70%. That doesn't mean that individuals have a 60-70% chance of having this disease. It just means that, of all the types of dementias that are possible, the "pool" of individuals who have a dementing illness includes 60-70% of individuals with Alzheimer's disease.

Without access to genetic testing, family history and age are the strongest indicators for a potential diagnosis of Alzheimer's disease. More specifically, the likelihood of having Alzheimer's disease increases with age. Among those over 65, the risk is approximately 1 in 10. For those over 85, it is approximately 1 in 2.

Other dementing illnesses, most notably vascular, can be more readily diagnosed with head imaging studies. Vascular dementia, which is often related to stroke, is the second most likely type of dementia.

Recognizing signs:

For most people, the first sign of Alzheimer's in a loved one is what we might call a "glitch." Slight forgetfulness – a mislaid checkbook, a missed appointment, or a forgotten phone number – may be what we notice, or, perhaps more to the point, what we notice happening with worrisome frequency. At first, such failings are easy to dismiss. We tell ourselves: Who wouldn't forget a dentist appointment? What do we expect from a 92 year old? More accurately though, who wouldn't *want* to forget a dentist appointment? In truth, although it is in our nature to make excuses, to look for reasons, we do *not* forget our appointments with any type of regularity, regardless of how potentially tormenting they might be.

These first signs may be recognized by a caregiver, a family doctor, or a social worker. But even if a trusted healthcare professional raises the idea of a cognitive decline, some family members will quickly and summarily dismiss any potential diagnosis as "normal aging." Some people simply are not knowledgeable, and so do not understand the implications of the disease. Others do not want to hear it. Such reactions often fit neatly with the first impulse of the declining person as well. After all, one of the most common responses of people who are experiencing cognitive decline is denial, dismissing the concern as unwarranted, the triggering event as trivial. (The other response, worry or depression, can actually be healthier, allowing both the person and the family member to accept and work through the issues associated with such decline.)

When there is confusion or denial, anger and resentment often follow. Just as my dad would complain about my mother, saying that "she's doing this to me," so may others who do not understand or accept the neurological nature of the decline see the new or aberrant behavior as a choice, a personal attack. After a while, when the "mistakes" become a bit more obvious and frequent, the frustration starts to build. The relationship becomes more strained. "Let's go see a doctor" is answered with anger: "You think I'm crazy? You're just trying to get rid of me." Adult children and even spouses commonly experience such responses. "You'll get your money soon enough."

Ironically, such reactions can be a great barometer in helping the caregiver judge reality. As evidenced by my own experience at that long-ago dinner, caregivers often react to stress with anger or frustration. The pressure is rising. Without awareness of what is happening, caregivers tend to blame themselves. The caregiver will commonly lament "is there is something wrong with me?" Caregivers assume that they have a responsibility to care for their loved ones. They assume they have the entire responsibility for righting the situation. I was lucky, in that I have the professional experience to know otherwise. For caregivers who are not professionals, such an expert opinion often only comes when the stress becomes too great or some crisis is reached and a doctor or other professional is finally brought in. But such crises, instead of being "breaking points," can be lifesavers. Once the caregiver seeks assistance, she becomes aware that the problem is rooted in her loved one's disease, and the focus is appropriately shifted.

Harold, for example, is a gentle man, a retired optometrist, and also the caregiver of his wife Marie, whose disease he became aware of several years prior to our first visit. He is intelligent, thoughtful, and sensitive, but when we first spoke it became clear that he did not have a clear sense of how cognitively impaired his wife had become. I asked Harold to assess her cognitive functioning, using very simple questions. We discussed her ability to meaningfully process information, and even whether she recognized familiar people in her life. Harold readily reported her decline, but still struggled to accept the level and impact of her impairment.

For the longest time, Harold still took Marie out to dinner. But because he both denied her real condition to himself and tried to hide it from others, these evenings out had ceased to be pleasurable. Instead of accepting the reality of her cognitive impairment, he would, instead, feel embarrassed when she walked over to other tables and start chatting with strangers. He asked her why she did this, but he seemed to know in advance what she would say. She "feels connected" to those other people, she would tell him, in ways that he simply didn't understand.

For years, Harold tried to joke such behavior away. "She just loves babies," he'd say, if the strangers had a child with them. Meanwhile, ironically, Marie would be apologizing for his "standoffish" behavior.

Esther, too, found herself conjuring up explanations for her husband's behavior. Long after he had moved into a nursing home, Harvey still spoke about selling his business. There was no concrete business to sell, she would explain with mixed emotions. It was more of an idea. This was a sore subject for her, one that caused her great frustration, as he would expect her to participate in facilitating this process.

Harvey would speak about this "business" to all who would listen. He was a proud man, highly educated, and refined. His "business" was his identity. But for Esther, it was an albatross. Whenever he brought it up, she would try to shift the conversation, in whichever context it occurred, all along smiling and pleasant. She would try to deflect his obsession, suggesting that "people don't want to talk business," when the truth was that people felt awkward trying to understand his so-called business or his potential efforts to sell it. Even when Esther knew nothing could be done, she experienced the pangs of frustration. A good wife, loyal and loving, she wanted to be there for him, to appease his anxiety and help him in his quest to achieve his goal, no matter how fruitless.

Unwilling, and too genteel, to express what must have been her growing frustration as anger, she compensated instead, throwing herself into a caregiving role that may not have been necessary – and complaining, gently, that with all that she had to do to care for him, it never seemed to end. At the end, she simply appeased him, until the requests ceased. Esther's strategy at the time was not what they had chosen, together, when Harvey was in his "cognitive" prime. Before his decline, their goal was to work together to create a healthy compromise on issues of concern. However, at this later stage, with Harvey's decline, immersing herself in the caregiver role seemed to suit her best.

Helen was lucky. At her request, she was referred to me through her primary physician fairly early on, and so she was able to recognize and work with her husband's behaviors. Initially she observed herself getting frustrated because he would ask questions. Too many questions. Irrelevant questions. Questions that were not timely. Worse than his questions were his expectations. He expected her to respond and address his concerns immediately, to answer questions about bills, taxes, the mail. Even when she did respond, he would ask these same questions again, or wonder why she had not addressed his concern sooner – even when she had.

Helen was quite similar to Esther in many ways: genteel, always well put together, and a firm believer in her commitment to her marriage, to being a good wife. When her husband persisted, "demanding" a response or resolution to a problem or issue, she behaved as a caring wife would. She was dutiful, not in a subjugated way, but as a woman who took her vow – "in sickness and in health" – seriously. But she was human, and it became frustrating when he would ask the same questions over and over, or ask her to repeat or clarify something she had already responded to. She tried to justify this combination of obsession and failing memory to herself and to others as a product of his failing hearing. And yet, even when she spoke directly to his ear, the questions persisted.

I asked her, on occasion, whether she and her husband socialized. She would smile quietly, knowingly, aware of where the conversation was headed. Yes, she told me, they would occasionally go out and visit with friends. But even when he was well, her husband was not much for socializing. He was never the talker. Once he started to decline, however, this natural inclination became more pronounced. When they would visit friends, he would mostly sit and stare. When their friends and colleagues would inquire, Helen would cover. He was "fine," she would say. Just, again, "never much of a talker."

Helen knew she was not being entirely accurate, but it was easier than explaining that his mind was struggling to handle the interactions necessary to socialize. At some level, at least initially, she herself did not understand or accept that much of his behavior had to do with his declining ability to understand all that was going on around him. In the therapy process she began to recognize that these demands, while originating in his personality style, were now based primarily in his struggle to process and understand new information. And still, she would invariably react when the questions repeated themselves, especially when she felt overwhelmed by her other daily chores – or her sense of obligation toward him as a loving wife. It's one thing to listen to someone ask the same question on a good day. It is quite another, more difficult, challenge when you are overwhelmed with daily commitments, with paperwork, laundry, cleaning chores, shopping. Even when he went to sleep, she would awaken in the middle of the night, thinking, almost obsessing, about how to plan her next day. Even when she accepted, intellectually, what was happening with him. Even once she learned that his behaviors were rooted in his cognitive decline, she would find herself responding reflexively. Too easily, she found herself jumping to answer, to comfort, and to explain his odd, "standoffish" behavior to others, saying, "He was always this way, I don't expect that would change."

It is the rare family member, caregiver or loved one who can readily accept these changes. Harder still is it for both the declining person and those around him or her to look ahead, to face the future, and to consider treatment and living options.

Helen asked for my services because she found herself struggling to cope with her husband. She was unclear as to what exactly was going on, but she knew that her tolerance for his behavior was declining, and she found herself more and more frustrated by the simplest acts or questions. During our first meeting we spoke about her observations of her husband. Through methodical questions, she was able to accurately assess that his cognition had declined. This was truly a revelation for her. Before we went through these questions, she had assumed that his inability to act or to understand was just part of his personality. After all, he could be stubborn.

We arrived at this point through a series of small steps that led her to understand what was happening, allowing her to gradually accept it all. I asked basic questions that required her to think about what she thought she knew. Was her husband's memory truly intact, or was she assuming that it was? I gave her a simple exercise: ask her husband to remember three words in three minutes. She did, and he recalled only one. She noted that he often asked her to repeat questions, feigning what appeared to be selectively poor hearing. When I suggested that she speak directly toward him, so as to avoid the possibility of poor hearing, she recognized that his hearing was not the issue. Rather, his request for repetition was a compensatory strategy designed to "give him time" to think and process, or better yet, get her to facilitate by rephrasing or clarifying her questions and statements.

Helen was a quick and willing student. She recognized something was wrong, and for her, this knowledge freed her to sigh with relief. A loyal and loving wife, she wanted to understand her husband's condition. By doing so, she was in a better position to help herself. She was the type of client you cherish. Personal growth was her goal. Helping her husband was the natural end result.

CHAPTER 3.

$\mathcal{D}$iagnosis

My mother has *never* been formally diagnosed with Alzheimer's disease. That is, she has never been diagnosed by any professional other than myself, and my assessment is not based on any formal testing.

I write the above and am astonished. Although I know I write the truth, the above is nearly incomprehensible to me, given the amount of doctoring she has had over the past eight or so years. If anything, the amount of care she has required, and received, has obscured what, to me, is an obvious diagnosis.

In 2002, my parents moved from New York City to New Jersey to be closer to their grandchildren. That November, my father was in a car accident. He was driving, with my mother riding as a passenger beside him. As I understand it, the accident wasn't severe. He was pulling out of a gas station into traffic and was sideswiped by an oncoming car.

"He came out of nowhere," was all my father would say when I saw him that evening. He was hospitalized with a broken leg, and when I went to see him, he was as I'd expect. Hurt, angry, confused, maybe a little ashamed.

My mother ended up in a different hospital, and by the time I went to see her it was close to midnight. I was anxious about how she would respond and wondered why she had been transported to a different hospital. I wanted to see her and to talk with her. But when I got up to the hospital's front desk, I was not permitted in to her room. My mother left specific instructions that her children were not to be let in to see her. I was embarrassed, more than upset. I wasn't entirely surprised. I'm quite certain that our dynamics are not uncharacteristic of other parent-child relationships, at times loving, at times frustrating. As I stated earlier, she had a propensity for being moody at times. I wasn't sure what I had done "wrong," but I wrote it off as "just one of those moods." I turned around and went home. I reflect on this not because of some inner need for a Freudian release, but rather to demonstrate that our old pattern of behavior could easily be mistaken as par for the course if we do not pay closer attention. In retrospect, however, I believe this situation was related to a blend of early cognitive decline, and her personality style.

After the accident, as part of evaluation for the insurance claim, my mother was sent for a psychiatric evaluation. The psychiatrist who evaluated her subsequently treated her for depression, using medications as well as individual and group psychotherapy. She would later tell me that he spoke to her about her frustration and anger, about her sense of loss and resentment following the accident, as well as her relationships with her family. Because of my mother's desire for independence, she did not initially inform me of her work with the psychiatrist. It was only much later, almost at the end of her visits with the psychiatrist, when my parents requested that I become more involved, especially as related to her medical concerns. That's when I found out that the psychiatrist had diagnosed her memory deficits as being related to the accident.

I had some frustrations that the diagnosis she was given was associated with her accident, specifically that her cognitive deficits were correlated with potential, though undocumented, head trauma rather than the early stages of Alzheimer's. However, I felt that psychiatric intervention would potentially assist in that it allowed for additional outside intervention.

What that psychiatrist did not, perhaps could not, know, partially because he did not have access to an accurate history (in part due to my father's denial of my mother's early condition which led him to resist my advice and thus fail to convey her true condition to the psychiatrist), is that my mother's depression was not new. Yes, on one hand, it was fair to describe her as depressed, and it seems reasonable to assume that this condition had been exacerbated by the physical impact of the accident as well as by her declining memory, which she surely must have sensed by that time. But to ascribe her problems only to depression made it difficult to understand the broader, and at the time, almost "hidden" concern of her cognitive decline.

My mother's life outlook at times teetered between the glass being half empty and completely empty. While clearly not an optimist, at times she could be characterized as a hopeful pessimist. But with her psychiatrist, she had an opportunity to focus on her negative voice, her frustrations and resentment, her unrealized hopes and expectations for herself and her family. In all fairness, this somewhat negative world view could readily be characterized as depression. It certainly provided the kind of fodder with which mental health professionals work. Following an automobile accident, to hear bitterness and resentment could reasonably lead a psychiatrist to diagnose my mother with depression. Without my mother's direct input or insight from my father that such feelings were representative of my mother's longstanding outlook on life, a sense of injustice that reached far into her personal history, her psychiatrist would not reasonably be expected to assume another cause.

My mother was in treatment for some time, in both individual and group therapy. And yet, her depression did not substantially improve. Prior to the onset of her cognitive decline, describing her depression as "treatment resistant" would have been quite accurate. Once cognitive impairment was setting in, depression was no longer the only issue. The problem was the diagnosis. Was it depression or dementia?

Diagnostics

Auguste Deter was only 51 when Dr. Alois Alzheimer first saw her. The year was 1901, and Deter was a patient at the Frankfurt Asylum being treated for an odd assortment of behaviors and apparent short-term memory loss. Dr. Alzheimer, a psychiatrist and neuropathologist, was intrigued by her case and when she died, a short five years later, he performed an autopsy on her brain. He found abnormalities that he identified as amyloid "plaques" and neurofibrillary "tangles," now the defining traits of what was then called "pre-senile dementia." His research was credited as the first effort to meaningfully identify this disease, which would be named after him.

Those brain abnormalities – the amyloid "plaques" and neurofibrillary "tangles" – are still the defining traits of a formal diagnosis of Alzheimer's disease. But because such signs cannot be identified until after death, we use various acronyms to describe what seems to be the disease. For patients over the age of 65 who present with Alzheimer's-type symptoms, we use the acronym SDAT – Senile Dementia of the Alzheimer's Type. For those younger than 65 (fewer than 10 percent of affected individuals), the term is PSDAT – pre-senile dementia of the Alzheimer's Type.

Whatever the age of onset, generally speaking, the course of the disease is fairly consistent. Over approximately two to 12 years, due to the increased death of healthy brain cells, the disease causes cognitive function to decline. At first, this is noticeable in small mistakes. Memory slips. But as the disease progresses it affects more basic functions, from maintaining personal hygiene to dressing oneself and eating. Ultimately, it leaves the person *who may otherwise be physically healthy*, unable to function. Finally, it leads to death.

Diagnostics are improving, but our tools for predicting the disease remain somewhat limited. High-end imaging studies, such as MRI and PET scans, can see the pattern of impairment fairly accurately as the disease progresses, but usually not as well in the early stages, although some recent studies are suggesting improvement in early diagnostics using high powered imaging. A small study, done in 2006, used EEG brain wave data to accurately predict Alzheimer's disease 10 years prior to its onset. Gene testing, specifically testing for the apolipoprotein E-epsilon4 genotype, is also considered a strong indicator. But this test is usually done in research settings. For the general public, family history and age remain the best predictors of incipient Alzheimer's, and a variety of behavioral symptoms are the predominant means of diagnosing the disease in its early stages.

The First Step

Different types of dementia present in different ways. Individual patterns of cognition, behavior, and psychology present subtle clues, and by observing these differences a qualified clinician can usually make a reasonable diagnosis. There are areas of overlap. Memory loss, for example, may show up in various types of dementia, but clinicians with some expertise should be able to distinguish between vascular dementia, for example, and SDAT. One determining feature in this case would be whether the patient has ever had a stroke or any vascular risk factors. Such determinations become harder if the person has advanced cognitive impairment and has also had a stroke in the past. Then the clinician would need additional information, such as where the stroke occurred in the brain and whether its severity was enough to justify the level of cognitive and/or behavioral impairment. Other factors will have to be considered as well, as other forms of impairment may be superimposed on SDAT.

So how do I know that my mother has Alzheimer's' disease? Why do I doubt that her memory loss is significantly related to her automobile accident?

First, and most importantly, her memory loss predates the accident. This isn't recorded in any official document. She and my father tended to dismiss or discount any concerns. But in my profession as a geriatric psychologist, I am trained to see such things and to take note. Because I was alert, and because I know how the problem presents, as in her persistent forgetfulness and decline in organization skills, I recognized it early on.

Secondly, the accident was not serious. There was no clear indication of head injury. Furthermore, the kind of head injuries associated with memory loss or other lasting cognitive impact are generally those that come with loss of consciousness or serious trauma that can be seen in head imaging studies, neither of which she had. Over time, both her memory and cognitive abilities have clearly declined, and while it is possible that head trauma, even mild, may contribute, it is, in this case, not causal.

Finally, my mother's cognitive decline has been characteristic of what is called the "Alzheimer's triad." This triad of symptoms includes difficulty in encoding new information, subsequent recall of this information, and difficulty with language.

Let's look at those more closely. It's not uncommon, when talking with a person in the early or middle stages of Alzheimer's, to hear the comment, "My memory is perfect. I can remember things from 50 years ago." This may be absolutely true and yet still be inaccurate. As the first part of the triad makes clear, long-term recall of well learned information often remains quite intact Unfortunately, if you ask that same person what she had for dinner the night before, she likely will not remember. That's because the menu of the recent meal is new information, and one of the symptoms of Alzheimer's is that new information is not fully encoded into the brain – and thus cannot be retrieved later on.

Language difficulties are somewhat different. People often lament that they forget names. For example, a grandparent will go through several family names before arriving at the desired name for a particular grandchild. This doesn't necessarily indicate the beginnings of cognitive impairment. Language difficulties in the early stages of the disease are observed more commonly as a person's struggle with everyday language, such as when a person has difficulty coming up with the right word for an everyday item – the car keys or the refrigerator – or with a word that normally occurs in casual conversation.

Of course, not all language difficulties are indicative of Alzheimer's disease. We all suffer from occasional "tip of the tongue" syndrome, when we struggle to access a word or a memory that is usually quite commonplace. And more serious loss of language can be symptomatic of other health problems, such as TIA's (small or "mini" strokes) or even a full CVA (stroke). Depression and other psychiatric concerns can also affect language skills, and may be both treatable and transient. These and other possibilities should be considered in any evaluation of cognitive functioning. However, once other causes are ruled out, the pairing of language difficulties with memory deficits may be indicative of early Alzheimer's disease.

That said, my mother has demonstrated both symptoms of memory loss and declining language skills, and although she dismisses such forgetfulness as "normal," it is persistent, pervasive, and beyond the norm for someone of her level of education and functional abilities. It's one thing to be overwhelmed at work and to misplace papers. It is quite another to constantly forget items when there is no apparent external pressure – and then to blame others for those errors.

These symptoms can be scary and frustrating, both for the person struggling with the language and memory deficits and for the loved one trying to communicate. Some of us may resist acknowledging the level of deficit, convinced that we can spur or will our loved one into remembering. But family members and caregivers who repeatedly prompt their loved ones, saying "Don't you remember?" are fighting a losing battle. Their loved one doesn't remember, and will not be able to remember despite prompting because the nature of the disease is such that the person has been unable to process the information properly. And because the information has not been fully coded into the brain, the affected person will not be able to retrieve it, to "remember," no matter how much we coax them. "Don't you remember what I told you last night?" would be better rephrased as, "Last night, when we spoke, I mentioned to you that…" Ironically, it's not uncommon for family members or other caregivers to actually mask their loved one's decline by "ignoring" the reality of the memory loss. Perhaps such gaps remind us too much of our own mortality, perhaps our personality type simply struggles to accept these changes.

My mother, for example, blamed her loss of certain words, counter-intuitively, on her facility with language. She has been fluently multilingual since she was a child, speaking Hebrew and Yiddish, and English by the time she was in her twenties. When she struggles with words, therefore, she blames her multilingualism, the multiple vocabularies that she must keep straight in her head. The problem, of course, is that when she struggles, she cannot access *any* of the available languages in her head. For a person with her high level of intellect and functioning, this loss of language is significant. It is also, as with her other memory deficits, gradual, again indicative of a progressive degenerative disease rather than a sudden trauma, such as she might have experienced in the car accident.

The Next Step

My mother's psychiatrist diagnosed the primary cause of her memory impairment differently than I, principally because he had limited information. Why should that matter? Because the type of care and intervention depends on the diagnosis. The treatment is different. Memory loss due to a head injury or even due to a stroke, for example, may respond more directly to the type of rehabilitation known as cognitive remediation or cognitive rehabilitation. Think of this as physical therapy for the brain, allowing injured people to strengthen certain skills or develop other cognitive skills that can compensate for lost abilities. The most significant improvement with this kind of rehabilitation occurs in the early stages, shortly after the brain damage, with the potential for progress decreasing over time. In other words, someone who had a head injury or a stroke more than a year or two ago is less likely to benefit from this process.

Currently, cognitive rehabilitation is not generally recommended for people with Alzheimer's disease. Although some research suggests that such therapy, along with other factors such as genetics, and interventions, such as medication, can potentially help stave off cognitive decline for a limited period of time, it is more commonly used for those cases of a direct, serious, brain injury than a progressive, degenerative disease.

My mother never received the full evaluation her condition merited, partly due to the accident, and partly due to my parents' denial and reluctance to share personal information. The very early stage of my mother's decline, the chronology of which was superimposed by the accident, misled her psychiatrist because my mother, and for that matter my father, did not offer any additional insight. Given my level of expertise, I didn't need to perform a comprehensive evaluation. Unfortunately, such a "blessing" is not readily available to most people. As such, by far the most important recommendation I can make to any person who has any concern regarding their own, or their loved one's, cognitive functioning is to be completely forthright with your clinician and have a comprehensive cognitive evaluation performed. The input of an expert, an outsider who can objectively evaluate cognitive levels, is invaluable.

While the prospect of what may be found may be frightening, the evaluation itself is not overwhelming. Such an evaluation is not invasive. Patients are not required to disrobe or do anything physical, beyond the basic physical exam that a physician will do to assure that the patient is in good general health.

Instead, most evaluations begin with the clinician – preferably a geriatric physician, neurologist, geriatric psychologist or psychiatrist – asking questions. The clinician will thus gather a personal history, asking along the way about any family history that might be significant, such as "memory problems" or the like. This can be useful, because as recently as a generation ago, Alzheimer's disease was not readily diagnosed or recognized, and often a hereditary component of the disease can be hidden in family lore.

The family history will usually be followed by a medical history, which will include a review of the person's medications. The clinician might then ask several questions to gain a general assessment of the person's cognition. More a quiz than a test, these assessment tools serve as a screening, to give an overview. Often, they will involve pencil and paper tasks, as well as oral questions, designed to give the clinician an idea of the person's basic level of cognitive functioning. One such tool, the Folstein Mini Mental State Exam, is a 30-item assessment that examines several areas, including orientation, encoding of information, delayed recall, language and visual perception skills. Some questions might include asking the person to state the year, month, date and day, assessing general orientation to time. Another common question assessing for concentration might be to ask the person to count backwards from 100, subtracting by sevens, or spelling the word "WORLD" backwards. Finally, to assess delayed recall, a person might be asked to repeat three words, and later will be asked to recall them. The cognitive assessment generally lasts no more than 15 minutes. Some clinicians will add their own questions to a standard assessment, borrowing from different protocols or tests. Depending on the results, the overall score and the clinician's interpretation, the clinician may recommend further tests, such as brain imaging studies like MRI or PET scans.

These brain imaging studies may also reveal other underlying disease processes that may impact brain functioning. For example, normal pressure hydrocephaly, tumor, urinary tract infection, vitamin B-12 deficiency, or hypothyroidism are all medical conditions that may impair cognition. However, even the presence of such conditions can be misleading. A medical condition can, and often does, coexist with cognitive impairment, and misdiagnosis can mask the early stages of Alzheimer's disease. A person with hypothyroidism, for example, may have been living with the condition and taking medication for years. If that person subsequently develops dementia, it may have nothing to do with the hypothyroidism. If it did, then the cognitive impairment would likely have manifested itself closer to the time of the initial diagnosis of hypothyroidism, and treatment of the hypothyroidism would have likely improved the clinical presentation, the way the person acted, felt, and tested, and the same is true for other medical conditions.

Cognitive screening or brain imaging studies may be inconclusive. If early screening suggests that there is some cognitive impairment, a geriatric psychologist or a neuropsychologist can do a more in-depth assessment. Neuropsychologists have more extensive training in the functions of the brain, and greater familiarity with various disease processes. Using more detailed tools, including more extensive pencil and paper assessments, they may be able to more accurately measure cognitive strengths and levels of impairment, and give a more precise diagnosis.

It's important to note again here that "dementia" does not mean "crazy," and that these evaluations are not being done to see if a person is "crazy" or insane. When conducting an initial evaluation of a client, as I begin to ask questions about orientation to time or place, or who is the President of the United States, every so often the client will look at me, either with amusement or irritation, and say, "you know, I'm not crazy." My immediate response is direct and reassuring, "I know. I'm just assessing your memory."

We have mentioned this earlier, but it bears repeating. Such a misapprehension is not uncommon, especially for older people, because in the 1960's and likely before, the word "demented" was often misused to describe psychiatric patients, the severely mentally ill who were confined to institutions. Dementia is a neurological condition, one which primarily addresses the neuronal functions of the brain. People who are being evaluated and who may have some form of cognitive difficulties should be assured that they are not "crazy." They're being evaluated to see how their memory functions, and they should be informed of this. When my parents and my wife and I met to discuss the issue of estate planning, my mother blurted out a similar comment about the notion of her "sanity." She's a highly educated woman, but like others of her generation or even younger, she was misinformed. Dementia does not mean "crazy," and evaluations are not done to determine "sanity," rather, to assess cognitive functioning.

Usually, people do not come in for an evaluation alone. A family member, a loved one, or a friend often accompanies the person being assessed. This individual most likely knows the person being evaluated and has some familiarity with the issues at hand. This has both up and down sides.

The obvious positive effect is that the companion can provide objective feedback or insight. Often, people will minimize areas of concern and downplay their impairment, saying, "I do not leave the stove on!" or "I never get lost while driving." In such cases, having a trusted companion who can make sure the clinician is receiving accurate information can be invaluable. A third party can also be useful in providing, or correcting personal history, such as the number of children in a family, or what level of schooling the person being tested has achieved.

However, such a companion should be made aware of the need not to overstep. Sometimes, particularly if the relationship is close, the companion may have already assumed something like a caregiver role. Sometimes he or she becomes the spokesperson and can interfere with the ability of the person being evaluated to express herself. Particularly if there are language issues, the person being assessed may need time to express feelings, thoughts, or concerns, and a companion who may be used to facilitating communication should be careful not to disrupt this process. Additionally, a companion may unintentionally obscure the level of impairment. Due to impatience or a desire to facilitate, or to make the loved one appear more intelligent, a companion may answer a question, "fill in a blank" too quickly. Companions should try not to jump in. Either the person being tested will be able to answer the question in her own time, or she will not. This will not make the person appear "stupid." It will give the clinician the most accurate information about that person's condition.

To counter this trend, an effective clinician will usually let the companion know that he will have an opportunity to provide useful information – and then respectfully ask that certain questions be answered only by the person being evaluated. This is the only way to truly and effectively assess a person's level of functioning, abilities, and limitations.

Some points to consider when it's time to have a loved one evaluated or diagnosed.

o   Misdiagnoses are more likely to occur when a person is not seen by a qualified clinician, specifically someone trained to work with older adults. There are many people who work with older adults, but statistics suggest that only 10 percent of all U.S. medical schools offer formal educational programs or rotations in geriatric care. There are many ways to go about seeking a qualified professional:

o   You might first contact your primary care physician and ask for a referral for a geriatrician. She may not have a ready answer, but a couple of well-placed phone calls should give you the first contact.

o   Some health insurance companies offer a list of physicians by specialty, which is another starting point.

o   You might also call your local hospital and ask for the names of outpatient geriatric clinicians to whom they would comfortably refer patients.

o   If you do not have access to local professionals, consider contacting the Alzheimer's Association, who may put you in contact with the local chapter, which could further provide you with a referral list.

o   Finally, you might cautiously consider looking up resources on the internet, but consider the adage "more may be less", as this may lead you to become overwhelmed by information and resources.

I recently evaluated a woman at one of the residential facilities where I consult. My evaluation clearly indicated an advanced level of senile dementia of the Alzheimer's Type. When I spoke with her daughter to discuss the nature and extent of the disease, and its implications for her mother, I used the term dementia, specifically as related to Alzheimer's disease. She was surprised by the diagnosis. She knew her mother "wasn't doing well," but, still, my findings puzzled her. "That's funny," she told me. "Her doctor said she had Alzheimer's, but that he didn't think she had dementia."

In this case, either the primary physician was not fully versed in this area, or else communications between the physician and the family were unclear. There is no Alzheimer's without dementia. Dementia is the overarching term – the name of the book, the movie. Once a person's cognitive impairment reaches a certain threshold, generally when memory deficits are deemed to be pervasive and functionally impairing, all the diagnoses have the heading of dementia. What differs is which type of dementia. As mentioned previously, senile dementia of the Alzheimer's Type is the most common.

Many people, including some clinicians, are not familiar enough, maybe even unaware, of the difference. Some forms of dementia are somewhat similar and easy to misdiagnose. For example, fronto-temporal dementia is similar in some ways to Alzheimer's disease, in that memory deficits are common, and at times impairment in judgment and executive functions can be seen. Again, a perceptive, trained clinician, and effective assessment tools are necessary to distinguish between these diagnoses.

It is also possible to under-diagnose, primarily because of ageism. In other words, "it's normal to forget." Some people are what I refer to as "quietly dementing" in their homes and assisted living settings, simply because they have a routine that hasn't been broken, and therefore there has been no need for anyone to assess their cognitive functioning. Only when some significant event occurs – such as a hospitalization, or the hospitalization of a loved one who may also be a caregiver, or a change in residence – is that routine broken. Then, when the "quietly dementing" person has to deal with new information, and fails to process it, the decline becomes more apparent, and hopefully leads to an effective assessment and an accurate diagnosis.

When I noted before that my mother had never had her cognitive functioning formally tested, that wasn't completely accurate. After several years of psychiatric follow up, she was referred for an evaluation by a neuropsychologist. The evaluation was requested by the insurance company, to assess whether ongoing treatment related to her accident was justified. From what she later told me, it sounds like she was given some version of a mini-mental assessment. The neuropsychologist's report did not indicate that she had a full neuropsychological assessment. The findings indicated cognitive deficits that might limit her ability to fully benefit from ongoing psychiatric treatment. Because this assessment was related to her automobile accident, and, again, no other information was provided by my parents to the neuropsychologist, it did not go far enough to provide the diagnosis of Alzheimer's disease.

What does this mean? What are the implications?

Whenever my mother is hospitalized, as has become more frequent in the past few years, I now am more involved and inform the attending physician and nurses about her cognitive functioning. Initially, this process was uncomfortable for me. I felt like I was in some way "telling on her" and going against my father's inclination to minimize her problems. I had to actively shift to my role of a clinician. I am not "just" her son, but also a geriatric psychologist well versed in aspects of her disease. But this effort has paid off. Once the diagnosis became part of her "chart," it facilitated a more coordinated approach to her treatment.

Over time, as the frequencies of her hospitalization have increased and as her behavior has grown more challenging, with my mother refusing care or rejecting the idea that she needs treatment, my intervention – and my volunteering of information – has proven its worth. With the additional information, the caregiving "system" has become more effective. Recently, during a week-long hospital stay related to what was diagnosed as an ulcer, my father reported that my mother had posted numerous signs saying "No Visitors Allowed." Ironically, similar to the experience following her automobile accident, yet meaningfully different in that we now know that her behavior is not due primarily to her personality style, but rather to her cognitive decline and struggle to cope with dramatic changes.

My primary care physician, Dr. Hamels, is truly a wonderful person. This bear of a man is always gentle in tone and manner. He speaks in a very soft voice, sometimes too low to hear, and always wears a gentle and comforting smile. Unlike the contemporary image of the "power physician," bold and brash, he is collaborative. He suggests to me what a particular problem may be, and works in a calm fashion to rule out other options. He spends time talking with me and with his other patients.

At my request, Dr. Hamels also treats my parents. I knew when they arrived in New Jersey that his personality would suit them as well. My mother particularly likes him, especially the attention he readily and genuinely offers. I know he reciprocates these feelings, and therein lies the rub.

Some time ago, while visiting Dr. Hamels for some minor ailment of my own, he asked me about my family. As I've said, he's a caring doctor, and concerns himself with the entire life of the patient. And so, after catching him up on my immediate family, my life, and my work, I started talking about my mother. I told him how I observed her increasingly failing in both physical and cognitive functioning. An insightful man, he acknowledged her cognitive impairment and agreed with my diagnosis. However, at first, he disagreed with me about her level of impairment. She was not, based on his personal observations rather than any formal testing or assessment, as impaired as I believed. After we spoke some more, and I pointed out behaviors that were consistent with a more significant level of cognitive impairment, he came to see her as I do, and not simply as she would wish to be viewed. Through discussion and increased awareness, together we developed a collaborative approach that serves my mother's needs and true best interest.

My ongoing task as a family member, but more importantly as a professional, is to continually provide what I view as accurate and complete information to her health care professionals. This is the only way I know to help them gain perspective that will ultimately result in better and more comprehensive care for her.

About a year ago, my mother asked me to talk to a neurosurgeon about her ongoing neck pain. She was considering surgery, and wanted my opinion about what its efficacy – and its safety – would be.

I spoke with the surgeon, who explained that she did have some degeneration in her spine and that this could be causing her discomfort. Because I thought he should know, I told him about her cognitive impairment and my diagnosis of her. I particularly wanted to know his thoughts as to whether her cognitive impairment might affect her recovery from the surgery, as well as the original complaint itself. He was quite open and receptive to discussing this. Ultimately, he said, he felt that my mother's physical recovery would proceed unhampered, that it would not be hindered by her Alzheimer's disease.

I remained cautious, even skeptical, but my mother chose to go ahead with the procedure. It didn't work. That is, she recovered from the surgery, but the pain she complained of persisted. The neurosurgeon seemed honestly perplexed, telling me that the rate of recovery with such a procedure is usually fairly high. But what clinicians and loved ones often fail to understand is that Alzheimer's disease may affect a person's perception of her functioning. It may create a lower threshold for pain and a higher perception of distress – such as ongoing neck pain – that may not be readily explained based on her actual physical condition. According to the neurosurgeon, the pain should have been gone. But to my mother's impaired brain, it persisted, and she blamed the surgery.

Such a misperception, or difference in perceptions, is only one way in which this disease affects overall health care, and why accurate diagnosis and understanding of Alzheimer's disease is extremely important in helping individuals, caregivers, healthcare professionals, and care providers cope more effectively with the disease and its intertwined branches. Once the disease becomes a prevalent part of one's life, every other aspect of that life will be affected.

Chapter 4.

Early Days/Becoming a Caregiver

I miss my mother. Very much. This writing helps, but I truly can say that as the days, weeks, months go by, and I see the image of the disease that is enveloping her, I remember less and less of her. Her vibrancy, her intelligence, yes, even her sometimes "know it all" demeanor. In moments like this I wish I could be her son again, not the person I have become…a care provider.

I grew up being "parentified." From a young age, I was praised as "all grown up," the "little man" who helped with chores not because I had to, but because it felt right. Not because the adults in my house, my parents, had imposed such duties on me as chores, but because they were simply what I did. I liked it. It gave a sense of accomplishment and won me my parents' appreciation. Unlike kids who get "paid" for chores, I had no "chores" per se. I helped because I received praise and it felt good. Part of my life.

Therefore, caring, now, for my aging mother – for both my parents, really – feels natural. A return to my earliest youth. Every time I come over to my parents' home, I do some landscaping work, which started out as just "cleaning up" the backyard and has now become a "project" of actually beautifying the home. When I go inside, my instinct is to make sure "everything's okay." Is everything in place? Anything need arranging, or even re-arranging? I made arrangements for a cleaning person and a lawn service, both of whom come bi-weekly. Now if only I came in once every two weeks....

It is important to note here that there are gradations of caregivers. Although I am the professional, the one with professional expertise with my mother's disease, I am not my mother's primary caregiver. My father is my mother's ultimate caregiver. I am more of a helper, a support system, facilitating her needs, providing resources when appropriate and necessary – as well as professional expertise and guidance.

Taking care of my mother, and at times my father, feels natural, not unlike the work I do in my role as a geriatric psychologist. In both roles my goal is to provide support in order to maximize the person's potential. Somehow, because I am a psychologist and provide clinical services for others every day, I erroneously believed that my partial caregiver role for my mother would be easy. I certainly thought it would be easier. Perhaps because I seemed to be comfortable with the notion of responsibility in my early years I assumed this caregiving role would fit my self image.

When I first began to notice the decline in my mother's memory, I felt like I was seeing my destiny. I jumped at the chance to be my mother's, my parents', caregiver, knowing that this would win me forever the role of being "my mother's son." Finally, I would be able to prove my worth. All those years of education and practice, of becoming a psychologist and caring for literally thousands of strangers would finally "pay off." My emotional range, as well as my intellectual prowess, would finally be put to personal use. Caring for my mother would be the fulfillment of all that work, all that practice.

I wanted to dive right in, but despite those first few missteps – described earlier – I had enough experience to know that this is not always the best way. Rather than overwhelm my mother and father with information about her disease, I tried to gently provide them with information. At first, I spoke in generalities about aging and memory loss. I pointed out her tendency to write notes and then misplace them, to write notes and then write them again, to write notes and then not know why. When she dismissed these comments as the ranting of a child, I didn't push. I suggested she look around her, ask others, Evelyn specifically, if she ever experienced memory gaps. She wouldn't do this, because it was "too personal" to share with anyone. (This is actually a very common reaction on the part of individuals who might be struggling with early memory loss, or even their loved ones. Asking questions or sharing their experience somehow seems to imply a "failing.") Since "random" note taking was not particularly helpful, I suggested a more organized use of a small notebook, one that would comfortably fit in her pocketbook, as this she would be able to keep with her at all times. I suggested that she keep all of her medications in one spot, and even consider getting a pill box (she did not, as this was what "old people" do). I guided her in how I thought she would best take care of herself.

Initially, when I first started trying to reach out and my parents rejected my help, I was still an unseasoned care provider. I lacked the level of finesse I now have. To me, knowing the right thing to do was as good as doing the right thing. I was riding the fence between being a professional and being a family care provider. The two are not often intertwined, and trying to do both requires awareness of the separate roles, as well as skill in effective communication. When I spoke with my parents, offered support and knowledge, I was often quickly rebuffed. Not because of the content, necessarily, but rather because it was me.

My parents would not have treated an independent professional this way. The problem was that, despite all of my education and experience, my parents didn't view me as a healthcare professional, but rather, simply their son. Being a family member or loved one offering help can be quite daunting, requiring both sides to gain sensitivity as to the ultimate goal. My parents were brisk, at times even harsh. Over time, I grew to better understand and separate my role. Despite being viewed as the "child," I knew my role was more that of the professional, and as such I resisted the impulse to react. So I would watch them, especially my mother, struggling, and again reach out to help with a suggestion or a quick comment. Small steps. Depending on their state of mind, these were either received or not. When it was not, it felt like Chinese water torture. Each drip on its own was not so bad, but the accumulation of them wears you down, completely, to the bones.

Being a care provider, even a secondary one, is difficult. As I experienced, at times it can seem ridiculously daunting. But it is a necessary task, and one which many people choose to take on.

As we look at the role of caregivers – care providers – we see a variety of reactions. What is important to remember, for those of us who are professionals and for family caregivers, is the motivation at work here. A caregiver's tasks can seem thankless, the help unwanted, the advice rejected. Those reaching out may be reviled as busy bodies or worse. But beneath it all, most caregivers share the same motivation. When you speak to most care providers you hear it. At the core, they truly desire to help. Regardless of how healthy or otherwise a relationship may have been, once the care provider makes the decision, despite the struggles, she remains committed.

Not everyone initially embraces the role of caregiver. Some accept it reluctantly, as another burden in a busy life. Possibly as a confirmation of our parents' or spouse's aging, and thus, of our own eventual decline and death. Some come to this role with a history of interpersonal difficulty. For those who have had troubled relations when their loved ones (spouse, parent) were well, donning the caregiver role can be even more painful. It can feel like quite a burden at times, an area of unresolved conflict that can persist, sometimes even beyond the passing of the loved one, if it isn't acknowledged and addressed.

If you can gain distance, now is the time to give up those conflicts. In many cases, the idea of resolution changes. At this point, you and your loved one are not really resolving conflict, you are shifting your understanding of your loved one and her limitations to address issues, and as such, the conflict subsides.

When you view your loved one as she is, as I have worked persistently to do with my mother, you are really moving beyond your past. She is not truly "your mother" any more. She is a person for whom you care. It is a difficult process, which takes time and effort. I still struggle with the impulse to say "well, that's just my mother" because vestiges of her behavior and personality style are still there. But as the disease progresses, I know that even with that, her behavior is now guided primarily by her dementia, *not* by her psyche.

Most people, however, initially come to the role of caregiver with energy, if not enthusiasm. Sometimes, that energy springs from misguided optimism – the idea that because you are now involved, you will somehow be able to reverse the effects of the disease and "save" your loved one. Too often, caregivers cast themselves in the roles of messiahs, convinced that in doing all you can for your loved one, you will be able to save him. This is a way of staving off reality, pitting yourself against disease and time. Plus, it gives you the illusion of control: If you only work harder, you will succeed. If you don't, it isn't that the progress of the disease is unstoppable. It is instead that you haven't worked hard enough – a factor that you can control. And so you throw yourself in even deeper.

But I digress. When we first assume the role of caregiver, we usually do so with a natural energy. I certainly did, and focused first on doing what I could to assure that my mother's external world was secure. I facilitated setting up a power of attorney and drawing up a living will. I spoke with her primary care physician and I discussed with her the issue of long-term care insurance. I worked at educating my father about the disease, and tried to break down the dual obstacles of denial and lack of knowledge by presenting information, facts, and resources.

However well intentioned this plan was, it initially didn't work. I had fallen into a common trap. I was spending all my energy taking care *of* my mother. And I completely neglected to care about her. In all my bustling *about*, making plans and organizing meetings, I focused more on quantity versus quality. More of the here and now, less of what she hoped for or desired to have in her life and in her future. My parents moved to New Jersey to "be near the grandchildren." But while focusing on what they were moving toward, they neglected to address what they had left behind. Taking my mother out of New York left her isolated and dependent. No transportation beyond my father; no ability to enjoy the hustle and bustle that she had been a part of for thirty years in New York City. I had assumed that here we are, let's make the best of it, ignoring that she was still wishing for the ways things used to be. She wanted to be back in New York City, going out to dinner, a museum, a show, and here I was talking long term care insurance. Now that's a dichotomy.

This is a common mistake. We get so involved in the practicalities, the plans, that we overlook the person. We don't do this because we don't care. I certainly cared. It was simply that we ramp up too fast, we go from step 1 to step 10 in the blink of an eye, eager to set the world in order. In some ways, we become detached from the person, perhaps because it is easier and less painful. We look at the disease and plan for contingencies, instead of seeing the person and working with experiences.

In my case, this mistake was made easier because of my professional knowledge. It was all too easy for me to step into this role, the planner and organizer, but this jumping-in actually created more work. I needed to step back. To re-engage with my mother and allow myself to do the much more painful work of anticipatory grieving. What I needed to do was learn to be a true caregiver.

Sometimes, we make the opposite mistake. Instead of throwing ourselves into solving the "problem" of the disease, we throw ourselves into being the caregiver – and give up any identity outside that role.

This happened with one of my clients, whom I'll call Herman. Herman was his wife's husband, his identity defined by his role in her life. In their earlier, healthy years, that worked out for them. Ruth ran the household, acting as his mother as much as his mate. She took care of the finances, parenting their children, managing their social schedule. Everything.

And then she became ill. And just as Herman's life had been defined by Ruth's when she was well, so too it became defined by her now. He threw himself into the role of caregiver so that even as she declined, he could continue to exist around her. This didn't stop the progression of the disease, but it took him away from his real feelings for her, not only his fear and grief as he watched his beloved slip away, but also from the real love he felt and could have been sharing with her.

He wanted to save her. This is certainly understandable, and, if nothing else, shows the depth of his dedication. But it wasn't healthy, for either of them. I came to know Herman when his wife had finally declined to the point where she needed nursing home care. Even then, he over-managed, visiting every day and staying all day, supervising her care. Making sure she was receiving proper therapy and treatment. Feeding her, changing her clothing, and even bathing her. It was an exhausting regimen, and one that didn't allow the professionals at the nursing home to do their work effectively. It was, in brief, unhealthy. At some level, Herman believed that he could keep Ruth through sheer force of will. He wouldn't let her go, couldn't. But even a loving and strong-willed husband as Herman could not stave off the inevitable.

With my help, through the therapy process, which was part education, part grieving, Herman learned to let go a little bit at a time. To step back from his all-consuming role as care provider and simply be her husband. Through ongoing counseling that challenged both his behavior and his real motives for wanting to avoid his feelings, he was able to reclaim something of his former life, to reclaim his role as Ruth's husband and to truly be there with her as Ruth slipped away. I encouraged him to start participating in outside activities as well. He started going to the local Senior Center more regularly, made monthly contributions to his favorite Atlantic City casinos, and met with old work buddies. More recently, he started playing cards and visiting more frequently with other family members.

Again, the root of this problem stems from fear, grief, and confusion. Particularly at the beginning of this process, when we first step into our loved one's life in our new role, we are confused. Afraid. And we want to do it right. We would rather immerse ourselves entirely in fixing the problem or saving the person rather than dealing with the complex emotions that this situation evokes. Only if we take a moment for ourselves, to recognize and accept our own emotions, can we really see and truly help our loved one.

Learning to grieve is the first thing any of us must do as we assume the role of caregiver. By accepting the reality of the disease, by allowing our emotions time to catch up with what has happened, we can learn to be more emotionally present – to see the person as well as the problem. Only then can we actually provide necessary care.

Many of us may be familiar with Elisabeth Kubler-Ross's stages of grief. Thinking about these stages, and how we work through them, can help us in these first steps toward becoming a caregiver. Keep in mind, however, that these stages are not static or even necessarily linear. They are, however, a useful concept to help us understand what we go through as we come to terms with our loved one's disease, a tool that will help us become a healthier and more effective care provider.

As outlined by Kubler-Ross, the stages of grief are as follows:

Denial. Denial takes so many forms. Many caregivers who came to me for an assessment of their loved one's cognitive functioning, summarily dismissed the diagnosis of Alzheimer's disease. How could such an insidious and deadly disease happen to their loved one? Blame the barer of the bad news. Not everyone, however, is inclined to dismiss the diagnosis, but, as is with the physical loss of a loved one, it seems unreal, literally "unbelievable." Education and information can be useful at this point. Rather than insisting that a loved one has Alzheimer's disease, it is our role as professionals to provide the caregiver with information about the disease and encourage them to look carefully at their loved one to see if the signs and symptoms make sense. While the caregiver initially might resist, as soon as she begins to review the conversation, she begins to open up and "see" the truth. Not "my" truth. Just "the truth."

Denial can take other forms. Often, the denial relates to the impact of the disease on the caregiver himself. My father's experience is one such example. A vibrant and energetic man, you can all but see the energy drain from him when he talks about caring for his wife. Rather than recognizing that she is suffering from a neurological disease, he uses denial as an ineffective coping tool. All too often, after a grueling weekend, when I reach out to talk with him, words have lost their meaning. He shuts down, physically and emotionally. People in this situation may be referred to support groups. Some initiate or reach out for other kinds of support. My father declines any such assistance. He struggles to view my mother's condition as it truly is, and consequently its grave impact on him.

Anger. "Why mom?" we may ask. This can change in a moment to "why me?" as the burdens and realities of caring for a person afflicted with Alzheimer's sink in. These feelings – whether you experience them as anger, frustration, mild annoyance, or pure rage – are common. At times, such feelings can make a caregiver lash out at the afflicted person. My father regularly would express anger about my mother, because of the suffering in his life that she is, unwillingly, causing.

Anger is difficult to deal with. It's a common response, maybe even a healthy one. Our lives are changing against our will. How can we just accept that? But when we, or those close to us, feel anger, we must help them vent and process it appropriately. You can't stop being angry, nor should you advise anyone else to just "let go" of her or his anger. Such attempts are not only futile, but they can damage relationships between the angry caregiver and other, less involved care providers, such as other family members or professionals. Instead, whether this anger is your own or something you are witnessing in a caregiver, try to view it as a natural reaction to grief and to loss of control. Find other ways of letting it out. Some people use exercise as a way of letting it out. Others are more verbal, talking about their anger to family, friends, or support groups. And still, there are those who shift their focus, tangentially, such as actually forming support groups to help others, or participating in action to foster change, either on the medical or political front.

Each of us needs to find our niche, but holding anger in, or worse, inappropriately venting it against those we love, will only perpetuate, rather than release it.

Bargaining. This is a quieter stage, less often openly manifested and more likely to be heard quietly, in the depths of despair. This is what is at work when we caregivers start making promises, offering to "do anything" to make our loved ones better. We may not say it out loud, but those of us who work with Alzheimer's patients see it in the eyes of caregivers and family members. The sadness, the pain. Caregivers are willing to trade anything for it to all be a bad dream. But there is no bargain to be made that will undo the damage or remove the disease. Far better to accept that this is simply a part of our grief, a part of all caregivers' grief. To help ease through this difficult phase, try focusing on being in the "here and now." Whether we are the caregiver, or we are helping someone close to us in this process, we can emphasize how important it is to be a part of a loved one's life, rather than placing all our energy in the less likely process of trying to "undo."

Depression. A significant number of caregivers, and certainly many of my patients have, on some level, experienced depression. Research tells us that caregivers suffer depression at approximately twice the rate of the general population. We may not express it as such. Herman, for example, would rarely acknowledge feeling sad. But still, the signs were clear: loss of appetite, poor sleep, loss of energy, lack of motivation, frustrations, and, at times, a sense of helplessness and hopelessness.

To cope with depression, or to help a caregiver, try to focus on satisfying the caregiver's needs. Although you may feel sad or even guilty (again, the "Why her" or "Why him?" of any survivor), you, too, have a right to live and a right to be happy. Try to understand that sadness is normal and that when it is expressed, it allows you to mourn – and move on. Not to move on, or away, as some might incorrectly interpret, from your loved one, but instead get ready to accept the reality of the situation - your loved one's ongoing cognitive decline and the shift from the person she was previously. Depression is not normal. Depression is stagnant, damaging, and ultimately unproductive.

Focusing on this last point can help us move past depression. Caregivers can often learn to grow beyond depression by realizing that healing is beneficial not only to the caregiver and other family members, but to the ill person as well. Caregivers need to recognize that, by caring for themselves, they will help to maintain the quality of life of their loved one. If you're the caregiver, try to understand that you must, first and foremost, care for yourself. After all, when you fly on an airplane, the flight attendant informs you that, in case of an emergency, place the oxygen on your mouth, then on those with you who are young or infirm, right? Bluntly put, if you are dead, you are of no use to those who rely on you.

Acceptance. Yes, the process of grieving does eventually come to an end, and this end is what we call "acceptance," which allows for healthy coexistence. Acceptance does not always imply happiness, but rather a sense that "things will be okay." Your sadness is bearable, your life will be different – but it will go on.

When you've reached this level, you can actually be a "better," truly healthier caregiver. You do the best you can, and let your loved one know that she is getting the best that love and strength can offer. You have done what I call "***grieving for the living***," the anticipatory grieving that will allow you to accept that your loved one is on a process that may bring about a psychological and neurological death before a physical death.

With acceptance, a caregiver can be more open to change and can create opportunities in ways that may not occur when the care provider remains resistant to accepting the disease. Acceptance allows for a healthy detachment. Instead of assuming the possibility that your loved one can achieve or maintain a higher level of functioning, instead of wasting energy in a futile fight against the disease, you begin to view your loved one as he or she truly is. In doing so, you become more receptive, and better able, to care for him or her. I hope I've reached this level, if not fully mastered it. I know my father hasn't. When my father finally recognizes that my mother is not "purposefully" forgetting, or turning back food at the restaurant, he will be able to accept her disease, and her, as she is now.

As we are doing the difficult emotional work of grieving, we may also want to consider the practical work of preparing to live with a disease. Now, when you are beginning to deal with the practicalities of the disease, it can be useful to understand some of the resources and options available.

The grieving process is very difficult to go through alone, even with a good network of family and friends. Most of us may benefit from the assistance of professionals, to help us through the stages of grief.

Support groups: Sharing can be palliative, but I caution caregivers to be mindful that not all support groups are alike. Structure is vital. A support group should not simply be a venting session. Good, well-moderated support groups are designed to help people express their experience, but also learn from others and to find an opportunity to move forward. If the sole function, intended or otherwise, is to allow people to vent, ultimately, the care provider will return to his home unsatisfied and ill-prepared to move on, and the temporary venting will have been for naught. Support groups can be wonderful if their guiding force is based on the premise of acceptance and forward momentum.

Counseling: Not everyone likes to share in an open forum. Some people are more comfortable in a one-on-one setting. Psycho-educational counseling can be extremely helpful. Part of the counseling process that I offer to my clients focuses on the stages and symptoms of the grieving process, to help them understand what they're feeling and why. This is supplemented by educational material to strengthen their understanding of the disease, demystifying the illness. Most of my clients find this helpful, because there is a lot of misinformation and misconceptions out there, and knowing the facts may alleviate their fears, as well as offer them realistic hope and understanding as to what to expect. When possible, seek a clinician who has specialized training in geriatric issues, because you don't simply want therapy for your grief – you also want more understanding of what you and your loved one will be facing.

The two concepts are intertwined. You need therapy for yourself, to help cope with grieving, the loss. But in order to meaningfully work through the grief it is important to recognize the loss based on your loved one's condition. Seeing that your loved one is no longer the person you knew helps in letting go. The most effective way of doing this is by understanding what she's going through, as well as what may continue to happen. She may be at the early stages, and so it's difficult to fully accept that she is changing. But, as with Herman, when we spoke about what he would likely see as his wife's condition declined, and later it happened, it was easier for him to then accept the change and accept the process of letting go.

For example, toward the end of Ruth's disease, Herman was struggling with staff at the nursing home, because he felt they were "refusing" to help her remain independent. He was adamant that she could, and should, because it was "good for her." I suggested to Herman that while I didn't disagree with his hopefulness for his wife, realistically, as the disease process was rapidly overtaking her, she would likely experience a more pronounced physical decline. Once he observed this for himself, it was "easier" for him to finally accept and let go, and further helped him to let go of his conflict with staff.

Financial and legal experts: Knowledgeable elder-law attorneys and financial planners do a great job of educating those involved, as well as facilitating the ability to maximize financial and other resources. A living will, a power of attorney, a financial plan of action – all of these are options you will want as time goes on and the disease progresses. In my local area, I have a good relationship with several elder-law attorneys who specialize in the issues encountered by older adults and their families. One such elder-law attorney actually has a social worker on staff, and this social worker works with the family to maximize resources, seek out more structured settings such as assisted living facilities, and maximize the loved-one's involvement within the community.

In considering the grieving process, consider the notion of reasonableness. At this point, all you need to do is gain reasonable knowledge and put forth reasonable effort. I reiterate "reasonable" because, as a group, caregivers are not reasonable. We want to do everything – or nothing. Throw ourselves into learning about the disease – or flee from it. Indulge our wildest emotions – or stifle them. By focusing on moderation, a little bit of learning, a little bit of trying, recognizing that the grieving process may take months not weeks or days, we can find a way to live, to care, and to still be ourselves.

Being reasonable will not allow us to conquer the disease. But it will reduce our anxiety over not knowing. Similarly, putting forth reasonable effort encourages us to review our efforts, and place them in proper perspective. It allows us to take steps to help in a way that doesn't drain us of all of our strength, remaining available, while at all times appreciating that we are not, nor are we expected to be, super-human.

Take your time. Process new realities. Your life, your role in your loved one's life, have both changed. Even if you want to rush in – or run away – take time to breathe. Take time to remember who you were before this crisis. Take time to do what you need to do in order to keep yourself sane, healthy, and strong.

CHAPTER 5.

Involving Your Loved One

When I was a young boy, I asked my mother what would I be when I grew up. Without hesitation she replied "a psychologist." Not the generic "doctor" response. I wonder if she sensed something. As far back as I can remember I always had a very strong bond with my grandparents, I always enjoyed listening to stories, helping out when I visited their home, and just being around them. During my childhood summers, I would spend many happy hours at my maternal grandparents' factory, where they made women's apparel, "working" at the little tasks they gave me. In my teens, my paternal grandfather developed what I now know was Alzheimer's disease. After the death of my grandmother, I would visit him daily during the summers, and he would tell me stories repeatedly, as if I had never heard them before. I recognized that something wasn't quite right, but I didn't have any understanding of the disease. I did have a strong sense of connection, and I willingly and wantingly sat and listened.

When I began to recognize the signs and symptoms of Alzheimer's in my mother, it was a bit of a flashback for me. There were times I wondered if she would end up like my grandfather: disconnected, in a nursing home. I remembered my uncle visiting my grandfather daily after work, and watching as he assumed the role of caregiver, his full plate of daily job and family obligations now being overwhelmed by the daily needs of his ailing father. Every time my grandfather didn't answer the phone, my uncle would have to leave work to check up on him. Would that be my father? Would it be me?

Initially, I almost reflexively dove in, as I was viewing the role of a caregiver as my destiny. Once I was able to step back, and to some extent reflect on my familial history, I slowed down. I wanted my distance; I'd worked hard to get it, and so instead I offered suggestions. I stood apart and extended help primarily as an expert, "the doctor" in my family lexicon. Only after my parents moved to New Jersey did I first take on the role of secondary caregiver, but even this happened in stages.

The first step was to address numerous financial and legal issues while my mother was still in the very early stages of cognitive decline and able to make decisions. The most important was to maximize her financial resources. We met with two lawyers and with my parents' financial advisor to discuss what would be the most beneficial steps to maximize their finances, keeping in mind the financial impact should my mother require long-term institutional care in the future. I didn't take over the role of managing my mother's finances, but rather, put her and my father in contact with people who would be able to advise them.

As my mother expressed no initial reservations or trepidations regarding addressing financial and legal issues, I naively assumed the process would be simple. The first step was to consider long-term care insurance. Neither of my parents understood that this was designed to maximize their assets in case of a prolonged decline that did not require hospitalization, but required a higher level of care than they could provide on their own, such as the care that would be provided in a nursing home or assisted living facility. After discussing this matter with several consultants, including their financial advisor, they eventually acceded to the process, though ultimately for naught, as my mother's application was rejected, due to the indications in her medical chart of memory loss, and my father only maintained his insurance for one year. In the current health care climate, financial advisors and elder-law attorneys recommend acquiring long-term care insurance when people are much younger than my parents, as early as their 50s, when premiums are more reasonable and the process of qualifying is easier.

The next step also seemed like it would be a cake walk, namely to have a lawyer prepare a healthcare power of attorney, a will, and a living will for my mother, a fairly standard and common process. The purpose of getting these legal documents while someone is still meaningfully able to understand and participate in the process is to be prepared both financially and medically for the time when the person's cognitive functioning declines. The power of attorney can be limited or comprehensive. It may address medical, legal, and/or financial issues, speaking on behalf of the person, generally in the event that the person is no longer able. The living will is similar, setting forth the person's wishes as related to specific medical circumstances, such as a choice not to resuscitate (with a document colloquially known as a DNR – or "do not resuscitate" – order) or hospitalize (a "do not hospitalize," or DNH order). Finally, a will sets forth the person's desires regarding his financial resources upon his death or incapacity (as would be the case in setting up a trust).

My mother's ultimate resistance to this process resulted from her being told by professionals such as the elder-law attorney and her financial advisor that she should give up financial control over her assets and allow someone else to make the decisions. Both her declining cognition and her denial about it combined to make it difficult for her to understand why she needed to cede control, why she should have a living will, or the value of a financial trust. To her mind, she was always going to be around to make her own decisions. She required numerous conversations and consultations with the lawyers and her financial advisors, in order to understand that the focus of the process was on the *future*. As long as she was capable, she would make her own decisions.

The problems arose when my mother began going through the paperwork. The intricacies of writing a will can challenge even the most astute person. Even though their attorney spent quite a bit of time explaining her recommendations to my parents, I found myself repeatedly clarifying points for them, at times because the details were complex, and at other times because of the language barrier. To an outsider, it would be easy to view me as over-involved, over-bearing, and domineering. At one point, as any good lawyer should and would do, their lawyer asked that I leave the room, to assure that my parents were making independent decisions. The only comforting point came in developing the living will. With the help of the lawyer, who went through the step-by-step process of the various decisions which may be addressed, my parents were clear and concise, and there were no issues of concern for them. What a relief.

When we speak of caregivers, we tend to view the role generically, but it's important to recognize that caregiving is a multi-tiered process. Primary, secondary, helper, and so on. All are involved in caring for their loved one, but on different levels and with different goals and expectations. My role thus far as been as a helper and secondary caregiver. I felt the need to get involved because both of my parents are aging. My father has taken on the main responsibility of caregiver. In some ways, this has been a natural progression: my father has always taken care of my mother. He is the epitome of a true caregiver and has been such ever since they were first married.

But hasn't my mother been independent? An educated career woman? Yes – and no. My mother does not cook. The old saw that she "cannot boil water" is a well-worn joke in our house. And although I don't mean to imply that as a young woman she couldn't handle her own affairs, the truth is that once she was married, she simply did not. My father took care of everything, from driving to balancing the checkbook. And so, the notion of my father now "becoming" the caregiver is a misnomer. What has happened is that this lifelong role has expanded, and it has now become painful. My father takes my mother to the doctor weekly, for various ailments. Her doctor prescribes medications, which my father lays out for her diligently and with care. But this care is not appreciated. Because of her cognitive deterioration, she is prone to sudden mood swings. She will turn on him, without warning, accusing him of not acting in her best interest. At times, she will even refuse her medications, which sets off a chain reaction as she finds herself in increased discomfort – and then blames my father for "not caring." But wait, wasn't he the one who told her to take the medications? I've learned to stop looking for rhyme and reason.

In some ways, my mother's personality style has complicated her – and my father's – understanding of the disease. Her at-times contentious outlook predates the disease. That's why many people dismiss the disease and say things like, "well, she was always like that." Anger is dismissed as "he was always a curmudgeon." Depression is dismissed as "she was always a negative sort." In fact, while in the past it would have been her personality style that was affecting their relationship, now the disease is the primary cause. She's not refusing medication because she "wants" to be angry at my father, because she feels belittled in some psychological way. It's because she struggles cognitively to understand what's going on, and when he "tells" her, the impulse, which isn't uncommon with individuals who are *not* aware of their limitations, is to fight back, to defend against perceived accusations of threats to her competence.

My father isn't the only one who has to deal with my mother's erratic behavior. Just the other day my wife, Tami, and I went out to dinner with my parents. It was a mixed experience, with my mother sending back the food she ordered because it was not what she ordered (it was). She ordered dessert and then refused to eat it, saying it was "too much" (which begs the question of why she ordered it). After dinner, Tami asked me if there are individuals who are aware of their condition and the extent of their memory deficits. The answer is an emphatic yes. There is no clear indication as to why some people are aware and receptive to understanding the process, while others may be aware and resistant or simply unaware. I guess the simple answer is that this is what makes the human being a distinct and unique entity.

Esther was a great example of someone who was aware of some memory decline and open to learning about the process. Although our work was not directly related to her memory loss, and in fact, it later became exclusively related to her husband's cognitive decline, she too noted that her short term memory was ever-so-slightly declining. Her observation was correct. She was exhibiting the earliest stages of the disease, but she knew what was happening and was willing and open to discussing both the implications of what she had found and possible treatment.

What made her willing to explore what must be a terrifying reality? My sense is that this openness and curiosity were part and parcel of who she was. A woman willing to consider alternatives, to explore aspects of her life. After all, she was the one who sought counseling for herself and her husband when I first met them. I acknowledged her concerns about her memory, and we spoke about specific ways she could address and compensate for her difficulties. Because she was receptive from the start, she also responded very positively to the use of coping strategies. She made a sign for the front door –"DON'T FORGET YOUR KEYS" – and posted a large calendar in the kitchen for important information. Her finances were already being addressed, so this was no longer an issue. We spoke about her driving, and she was well aware of the need to pay attention and make responsible decisions. She kept active throughout all the time I knew her, socially, cognitively, and with her family. She did everything she had done as a young person, and more importantly, as a person without Alzheimer's. The only difference for her is that she was now aware of her limitations and was working actively to minimize her difficulties, rather than ignore them. In every way, Esther is a model for an aging person confronting a significant obstacle with a healthy outlook.

Then there was the case of Helen. I've always thought that the world has a certain mirror image to it, and that in different times and places, you meet people who you would swear are related to, or may even be the identical person you had met some time before. I always thought that of Esther and Helen. Their personalities, disposition, outlook, and even physical presentations were so similar. And yet, in one very significant way, not similar at all. Helen also struggled a bit with memory loss, similar to Esther. Like Esther, Helen recognized her cognitive difficulty, and even briefly spoke of it. But unlike Esther, Helen dismissed her cognitive "gaps" as situational, blaming them on her struggles with her husband's admittedly more advanced condition. I never pushed the issue, primarily because she didn't appear to be psychologically ready to confront it directly. But in our sessions I did try to suggest that she might be experiencing some cognitive decline that was not related to stress. Her primary physician even recommended that she might undergo a neuropsychological evaluation to further assess and rule out Alzheimer's disease or other neurological disease. She declined. Always graciously and with the utmost respect.

It's curious to me why a woman who so readily accepted her husband's diagnosis, who was fairly well able to implement strategies to cope with his condition, would so completely reject similar understanding – and help – for herself. Though she never openly stated this, my sense was that for her, acknowledging the disease would have reflected a "failure." I also suspected that as she saw her husband decline, she feared that she would follow suit – a terrifying prospect, and one that would be difficult to acknowledge, even to herself. Instead, she focused on the disease as a "punishment." She had worked so hard to be good (she was) and strong (she was), and now this? We did discuss the notion that her husband's disease was not something she could control, but was something she could work with. She accepted that concept, but it was easier to externalize it as related to stressors as opposed to seeing it as a disease that was now a permanent part of her life.

My now infamous family dinner reminded me that not every person can be an Esther or even a Helen. When I told my mother that I believed she had Alzheimer's disease, she neither accepted the idea that she had memory loss or the specific disease. For some people, this diagnosis has the stigma of a fully dysfunctional person, sitting in the corner of a nursing home, in a wheelchair, drooling, oblivious to all that surrounds him. For others, it is a somewhat simpler, though still devastating view: one of impending death. They may not work through the steps leading to death, but they know that Alzheimer's means imminent death, and never one that is peaceful and dignified. They fail to recognize that people with Alzheimer's disease may pass away long before the disease progresses to its end-stage, and that people without Alzheimer's disease also die prematurely. The disease has such horrible connotations that the mere mention creates anxiety and distress.

Then there are those who associate the disease with the loss of control. At first, the loss is associated with the need to ask others for help, due to memory decline. Then the loss is associated with the need to ask for more extensive physical help. Finally, the loss is associated with the inability to make any decision, and having all that you have worked for and earned taken away: money, driving privileges, home, the right to make a decision about your well-being. These are not unreasonable fears. Unfortunately, in experiencing them at the early stages of the disease, or as a prelude to a diagnosis, we minimize our ability to maintain a productive quality of life. By anticipating and not fearing loss, we can act to defend against it, and in doing so, make choices that maximize our quality of life. We can seek others to assist in managing our finances, transfer our finances to others, move to a 55+ community, set forth in writing our health care desires for when we no longer are able to effectively communicate, all in the anticipation of what may come. Planning is healthy and reasonable, when it's done in the process of moving forward, and creating a forward momentum. It's stifling and de-valuing when it's done in fear of what has yet to, and may never come. Fear only serves to immobilize.

Part of my mother's reluctance, I'm sure, was the stigma. For too many, the diagnosis sounds like a mental health issue, as opposed to a neurological condition. Too often, it carries feelings of shame and of failure, the misperception that if only they had sufficient will power they could undo or conquer the disease.

The difference, as I've seen it throughout my practice, is actually rather straightforward. Although we are all individuals, and we all incorporate new knowledge in different ways, the ability to accept, and digest, such a diagnosis is usually paired with an ability to see the disease as just that: an illness. People who personalize Alzheimer's, seeing either shame or some moral failure in it, have the hardest time. Those who are overwhelmed by their fears of the future can have problems enjoying the present – or making plans for the future. But those who regard it as a simple, almost external fact – a thing that has fallen into their path and must be dealt with – are more readily open to understanding the impact of the disease and coping most effectively with it

How involved can we reasonably expect the loved one to be?

Because we are all individuals, there is no one simple answer to this question. Several factors play into involving the patient in his or her own care. Perhaps the most important is cognitive ability. Someone who is not significantly impaired may choose to become very involved. On the other hand, a person who is moderately to severely impaired will, more likely, not be able to be as significantly involved.

Another factor, not directly connected with cognitive ability, is awareness. Those who have some insight into the disease, some sense of it, may be more predisposed to be proactive and will make all attempts to help themselves. In Esther's case, her awareness prompted her to take action, and this helped her cope with her husband's cognitive limitations and make plans for herself.

Involving your loved one can be done simply and with dignity. At the early stages, ask questions, seek insight, and try to engage your loved one on every level possible. Obviously, questions that require information that he or she is unable to process may be difficult, and people who are cognitively impaired may make poor choices. Offer questions that are appropriate for your loved one's reduced abilities, and, if they are confusing, try reframing them to permit involvement. Instead of asking which medicine your loved one wants, for example, ask him or her to recount how medication helps maintain quality of life, and encourage her to take the prescribed medications.

No matter what the person's level of impairment or awareness, we should afford each individual the opportunity to be a part of his care. Try giving your loved one a say in his care, even if that say is simply a chance to express an opinion or feeling. Ask, and then wait for the reply. Simply listening, even if what he says does not make much sense or cannot be applied realistically, is a boon. Rather than being an empty gesture, such an airing allows us all to maintain a sense of humanity, of involvement in the process of living. It can also facilitate care as the situation changes.

Doris was a client of mine with very minimal short term memory difficulties. Everything else was essentially intact for her "eighty-something" year old brain. She was diagnosed with a terminal disease, and had a devil may care outlook on life. "I'm going to do what I want," she'd say, and I agreed. One of her frustrations was that her daughter wanted more control over her. Doris enjoyed driving, in limited fashion, but her daughter preferred that she didn't. There were no clear indications that Doris was driving unsafely, but I suggested that Doris and her daughter discuss the issue. My role was to help Doris maximize her potential while remaining reasonable and thoughtful. I encouraged her to be involved socially and physically, while accepting her periods of wanting to "just lay down and rest." Her daughter was trying to give care to a degree that at the time didn't yet seem necessary, and that did not take her mother's very strong personality into account. You need to be careful not to push too hard or too early. Trying to take over at a time when your loved one still has most of her faculties in place might ultimately result in your loved one pushing away.

The key here is keeping your loved one involved. At every stage, some level of engagement is possible, and keeps both us and our loved ones moving forward in a more positive way. In the early stages, having some say in care, treatment, or housing is a way of maintaining control, of still feeling like a competent adult, even as your loved one becomes aware that changes are occurring and that she may no longer be fully "in charge." As the process of cognitive decline progresses, encourage her involvement as a way to focus on her strengths and abilities. Finally, at the later stages, encourage involvement as means of maintaining dignity.

The obstacles to involvement really fall into two camps. The first, which we have touched upon, is ability: What *can* the person do to help determine or facilitate her own care? The second is the person's acceptance of her cognitive decline and the need for assistance. What does the person know she *cannot* do? Does she know she has a problem or that she is unable to fully do for herself?

What your loved one is able to do will vary from person to person, and from time to time within each person over time. People refer to having "good and bad days." Within each level of functioning, there is a range of abilities. At any given time your loved one may be better able to access compensatory skill sets. It is when he moves to the next plateau and the skills sets have failed completely, that he may no longer be able to assist or be involved as he was before.

Cognitive assessments, that is, neuropsychological evaluations, are a good first step, as are functional assessment protocols, usually filled out by the person and his primary caregiver. A neuropsychological assessment will help to gauge areas of functioning. For example, if a person's short and/or long term memory is significantly impaired, it is not likely that this person will be effective in managing appointments or even taking medications safely. This may be confirmed by the functional assessment tool, in which the caregiver will observe that the person struggles with new information, such as doctor's appointments or taking medication on time, or consistently. In such cases, clearly, the person cannot be solely involved in scheduling appointments or be left alone to manage his medications.

What a person *will* do may be more difficult to determine. At times, the nature of the disease may confuse the two. Particularly in the early phases of dementia, ability and awareness/willingness can become confused. Your loved one, for example, may believe that he can do more than is appropriate. He may resist offers of assistance, or actively react against them. When my mother, for example, resists my father's attempts to get her to take her medication, she is both resisting aid and fighting against the reality of her impairment. She neither wants to accept help, nor is she fully aware of the level of her cognitive impairment.

This can be difficult for loved ones and for their caregivers. My mother is constantly chastising my father for "telling me what to do." When he tells her to take her medications, she refuses, saying, "I took them already" when she had not. When he tells her she has a doctor's appointment she replies, indignant, "I know, you don't have to remind me." Or worse: "No, I don't," she'll say. "It's next week." And when my father corrects her by telling her what day of the week it is at that time, she first resists, and then concedes. At times this appears to be just matter of fact, and at times it almost appears that she is quietly suffering, though she has never said so.

The key is to pay close attention and facilitate without taking over. If the person is clearly making mistakes with his finances, make an observation and ask him if he might have some concerns. Hopefully if he is aware of the problem, he will ask for help. If not, you might need to intervene, gently but in a matter-of-fact fashion – what psychologists refer to as being low in "expressed emotion," or, more simply, drama. It is important to note that the issue is not about right or wrong, and keeping your observations value neutral can make them more palatable and easier for your loved one to accept.

This approach came to light in Doris's case. Ironically, Doris had subsequently reduced her driving significantly by her own choosing, recognizing that her physical decline may be compromising her safety. If Doris's daughter had pulled back a little more and just made suggestions and worked toward compromise, Doris may have been more open to her suggestions earlier.

Helen is a classic case of a person who would benefit from some assistance, but who struggles in accepting such help. She did have her son review her finances, but she insisted on remaining "in charge." When she pointed out that she "forgot" our appointment, she quickly dismissed this as related to "all the things I have to do in a day." While this seems reasonable, most of us are able to maintain a regular schedule and keep our appointments. When the "once in a while" slip up started to happen more frequently, it seemed that some assistance would be helpful. At the time I was visiting with her, she was not ready for this assistance. In fact, she was quite resistant, in her gentle and respectful way. It was too early to insist. She's lucky. She has a loving family who is aware of her limitations. They will help when the time is right.

A slightly different case, but somewhat helpful: Ms. Haroldson was accompanied to my office recently by a lawyer, her temporary guardian. Ms. Haroldson lives alone, but her neighbor had observed her decline, and reported her to Adult Protective Services. I was asked to assess what her level of functioning was, and to what extent she would be best either at home, with or without additional supervision and structure, or in a more structured environment, namely an assisted living facility. My findings were fairly clear. She was moderately impaired overall and most significantly struggled with short term memory loss. When asked as to why her neighbor may have had concerns, Ms. Haroldson offered a sense of discontent, but replied, "we worked it out. It's all better now." Nothing was worked out, as the neighbor had little to do with her beyond observing her reckless driving. In addition, we discovered that the bank tellers at her bank apparently had been helping her for some time maintain her finances.

She, however, had no insight into the depth of her problems. When I suggested an assisted living facility, she was adamantly opposed. She would hear nothing of it. She was fine. Physically in good shape, with a pleasant, social demeanor, she could see no need to go into an assisted living facility. The choice required a "systems" approach. Her temporary guardian would work to become her permanent guardian, and would assist in setting up daily in-home care. He furthered offer me an assurance of regular visits in which he would assess for tell-tale signs of change. At the first sign of further decline, he would initiate further review for an assisted living environment. This way, we worked with Ms. Haroldson's strengths and limitations – and her resistance – to create a cooperative arrangement, helping her to maximize her potential, if only for the time being.

Is it ever possible to involve a person with plans for future care, and if so, how? Is there a better way to approach this discussion than by saying, basically, "You're losing it and you are going to die"? Yes. However, to do so requires a proactive approach. These days, we thrive on information. Sometimes we are overloaded. However, in this case, more information may be better than less: the more we encourage people to become aware and involved, in every way, the more likely they will be receptive to taking steps for future possibilities. We have no problem considering our financial needs, for example, planning for retirement, but when it comes to our mental health, we dismiss it as a fight for the weak. Focus on Alzheimer's disease as just that, a disease, and one we should treat as we would diabetes, and high cholesterol. Take steps to educate your loved one and yourself, understand its potential causes and ways to minimize its negative impact.

Another example of involving the person shows how something as simple as choice can ease the transition, even when awareness may be at a minimum. Rhoda, diagnosed with dementia, was ultimately involved in choosing her assisted living residence. A confirmed urbanite, she saw and rejected some very nice places in the suburbs, rejecting them as "out in the boonies." But with her daughter's urging, she visited others and chose one that is in Cambridge, Massachusetts, "her" city, and close to everything. Of course, she very rarely leaves it now – and then only accompanied by her daughter or an aide – but to her this gave a sense of "less change." She's still in the city, with everything nearby, even if she can't avail herself of it. When a vacancy first occurred, she was very hesitant of going to "heaven's waiting room," as she called it, and let the first available apartment go. But by the time the second one became available, she was "tired," as she put it, of "housekeeping." Plus, she'd lost her driver's license. She was ready to go, and it was to a place of her choosing. Her daughter didn't "put" her anywhere, and so she was much more accepting.

Rhoda's choices were guided, and limited to safe options: she would move into one of the assistant living situations, but she got to decide which one. The process helped her get into a safe place, but with a sense of empowerment that made her trust in her daughter stronger, and made continuing care a little easier.

Sometimes, people simply will not accept care. When this happens, the standard we must adhere to is whether they're putting themselves, or others, at risk. If that's the case, then no matter what the person wants, we must morally and legally act.

For example, if an elderly relative refuses to give up a driver's license, a physician may report him to the Department of Motor Vehicles and the license will be taken away. There are other situations which are not so clear cut. Refusing medication may not always lead to "forcing" medication. Even cognitively impaired people may be allowed to make their own choices, even if we see those choices as unhealthy. Reflecting on a person's beliefs and choices in life is important before making a decision as to whether to force an issue.

Sometimes it's difficult to determine what the person may have wanted. A living will can help us determine a person's choices, as may input from people with whom he has shared a past. For example, a friend or relative may have heard the person say, "No matter what happens, never allow them to put me on a feeding tube," or something similar. A living will or any written process can indicate any medical issue that the person would like to address in his life. It is important to recognize that sometimes people will change their minds. For example, a person persistently and clearly states throughout his life that he does not want life-sustaining measures, At an advancing age he finds out that he has cancer. While his past outlook may suggest that he may choose to withhold active treatment, he might now change his mind if he also knows that his grandson is about to get married, or his granddaughter is about to have a baby. As such, it is vital for caregivers to stay informed. Understand what's going on in your loved one's life, and try to see how things may change.

We must always act to keep our loved ones, and those around us, safe. But even though it can be difficult, we must also continue to try to include the person, her wishes and his understanding of life, in mind. We must remember that we are making decisions for another human being, and respect her or his choices when we are making choices on her or his behalf.

CHAPTER 6.

The Condition Worsens

Alzheimer's disease is marked by change. Over time, that change is always for the worse. Although there is no set time line for the disease, it always progresses. Over a course that averages from two to 12 years, we see people go from those early, easily hidden or overlooked stages to what we call the "midstage," commonly at about five or six years, and through to the final, inevitable end. Of course, even within that broader outline, the timing for each stage is variable, and individuals progress through different stages at their own pace. There may be genetic factors determining the rate of the disease, that is, the rate of decline. One recent study actually suggests that individuals with a higher level of education may stave off the disease longer, but succumb faster once the disease takes hold. Only one thing is certain: with cognitive decline you will begin to see functional decline.

While various treatments can have a palliative effect, they don't last long. What we are talking about is delaying the inevitable, finding ways to slow the progress of the disease and maximize the quality time left to the individual and her family. With this in mind, it can be useful to note that there's another way in which change characterizes Alzheimer's disease. While stability and consistency can seem to slow the progress of the disease, external changes – a move, an accident, or a significant loss – do seem to bring on dramatic declines.

We have all heard it: "She was fine until *that* happened." We can fill in the blank, with "that" being the broken hip, the move to the nursing home, the loss of a spouse, or the hospital stay for a urinary tract infection. To some extent, this sudden catastrophic decline is an illusion. The person with Alzheimer's has been declining all along, and the crisis has merely revealed the extent of this decline to us. It has removed the structure and routine, the habit of long-ago-learned behaviors that sustained our loved one even as the disease had progressed. Plus, it has broken through our denial.

A couple of years ago, my father flew to Israel for my cousin's wedding. My mother was scheduled to go, and declined literally at the last minute, conjuring up a rationale that my father didn't want her to go. My father was committed to go, and so the plan was for me to check in on her daily. The first evening when he was gone, she called me no less that four or five times, the last time at 2 a.m., to ask what she should do about feeding the fish. The "fish" were koi that were in the small outside pond. They didn't require her to do anything, but she became fixated on them and on my father's absence. She repeatedly asked when my father would return, and each time I answered consistently and without distress that he would be back in a week. The rest of the week was quite debilitating. There were days when she walked out of the house and went to the neighbors, telling them she didn't know where her husband was, and asked to use their phone to call me, even though the phones in her home were functioning. Each time she called I assured her all was well. After a few days, she seemed to stabilize somewhat, but never returned to baseline, even after my father returned. That episode was a turning point, a wake-up call to me. My mother cannot be left alone any more, except for brief periods of time, such as if my father has to go out for errands or for a quick meal with my family and me, because she becomes easily distressed and confused, calling him repeatedly asking for his whereabouts. His trip didn't *cause* her decline, but did seem to hasten it.

That's what I saw when I was asked to visit Harriet at the request of her family members. Harriet had recently been admitted to a rehabilitation center after a hospital stay. She was disoriented and confused – and her relatives couldn't believe it.

"She'll be fine once we get her home," her daughter said, with all the conviction in the world. "It must have been the hospital."

It's always the same. Some acute change in circumstances, be it an environmental change such as a move, or an event, such as a hospitalization, seems to provoke a decline. In reality, they simply reveal the extent of the disease. The true cause of the decline is not the hospitalization, the change in environment, or some flaw in the care. It is Alzheimer's.

But while some of this effect, the sudden drop-off due to a change in the environment, may be illusory, the opposite may be true, too. A lack of change, particularly in the early stages of the disease, may lessen at least some of the impact as the disease starts to take hold. Basically, when there is no change, when there is stability and structure in the affected person's life, the system and the person affected work hand in hand to shore up the person's cognitive, emotional, medical, and interpersonal resources. The structures already existing in the person's life help, and it is possible that one of the reasons the disease seems to progress more hastily in its later stages is because not only the cognitive strengths of the individual, but also all these other resources, namely the caregivers, are being exhausted.

In other words, in the early stages, we can help shore up the individual by keeping her environment as structured as possible. Writing down information, keeping lists, all the techniques mentioned earlier can be put to use. But at some point – to use a very loose calculation, probably after five or six years – these techniques become notably less effective. The masking, that is, the "everyone forgets an appointment" or "if I didn't have so much on my plate," start to give way.

As cognitive impairment moves from mild to moderate, we can expect more behavioral difficulties. Whereas the initial stage of the disease primarily affects the ability to process *new* information, as the disease progresses, the struggle becomes more profound – concerning the ability to maintain pre-existing levels of functioning. At this point, diagnosis and prognosis are fairly clear, although the person involved and his caregivers may still deny the source and extent of these problems. In some ways, it is easy to look for different causes. After all, Alzheimer's disease is a disease of the brain. Every action, behavior, event, is in some way affected by brain functioning, and as brain functioning continues to decline it spreads to other parts of the brain and its impact grows. A person with Alzheimer's may lose the ability to manage his finances as basic errors in math may lead to more significant errors. The inability to remember when or how much of a medication to take may result in missed dosages – or overdoses. Forgetting that an oven has been left on may lead to a catastrophe.

The effect of the disease can seem like it comes from other sources. As the brain continues to fail, for example, balance and coordination problems may lead to unsteady walking or falls. Even the most common learned behaviors may no longer be taken for granted. As with so many aspects of this disease, such progression doesn't happen on a set timetable. Some people with the disease may pass into this mid-stage of the disease before or after others. There is no absolute time frame.

What can help, especially for family members and other caregivers, is to keep sight of the disease's far-reaching effects – and of the disease itself. If someone is having trouble moving about, getting out of bed, or even feeding himself, that's the disease. Too often, I hear frustrated caregivers blaming the person. "He can do it. He just doesn't want to." But this is far from the truth. The brain is shutting down and "want" or will have nothing to do with it. The person is not necessarily depressed or stubborn, he may just no longer recognize the concept, for example, of eating – or understand the visual representation of food. That's why, as the disease enters its mid-stage, we observe people falling more frequently or having other household accidents. Not eating or losing weight. "Refusing" care or medications. There's nothing maliciously willful about it, and it is now, as the individual declines, that we caregivers must make the extra effort to recognize the extent of the disease. No amount of challenging or encouragement, no reversing into old patterns will allow our loved one to assume his or her prior level of functioning.

While we may have been able to ignore the "casual forgetfulness" of the early stages of the disease, mid-stage is the time when we must pay attention. This transition may come about as a sudden and dramatic change, as when a crisis throws the impact of the illness into high gear. Or it may continue to be masked. Often, people who come into nursing homes for physical rehabilitation are deemed "resistant" or "depressed," because they are not following through on a physical therapy regimen. Only when a cognitive assessment has been done, and care providers discover that the person is struggling with "executive functioning" (i.e., the kinds of tasks that are controlled by the frontal lobe of the brain), is a more accurate assessment made. The person is not unwilling, but rather, incapable.

No matter how we discover that our loved one has slipped into this next stage – whether through an acute crisis or gradual realization, confirmed by a cognitive assessment – the requirements of this phase are more striking and demanding. At this point, she or he cannot return to independent life. Some kind of intervention is necessary. Although not all individuals struggle through to the final stages of this disease – stages when word choice may become difficult, when a significant portion of the brain has died, and recognition of family members may fail – anyone who reaches the mid-stage will also need our help.

The good news is that because Alzheimer's disease has received a significant amount of attention over the last decade, there are an increasing number of resources available both for information and practical help. In addition to the Alzheimer's Association, there are numerous Alzheimer's directories that provide informational resources about the disease, as well as practical resources, e.g. Meals on Wheels Programs and care managers, for individuals and care providers. Sources, such as the Family Caregivers Handbook, compiled by the MIT Workplace Center, helps with simple definitions and also with ideas for resources, many of them funded by private or public institutions.

Start with information. Knowledge helps reduce anxiety and fear. The more information you gain about the disease, the better able you might be to cope with it, personally or in helping your loved one. And make sure that you're getting good information by seeking credible sources, such as this book. There is some difference between working with older adults, and learning through formal education about the aging process. Hands-on experience can be invaluable, but often needs to be accompanied by reliable information.

Having gained reasonable knowledge, the next step is to seek practical resources. What kind and level of resources you will need will be determined by your loved one's level of impairment. Two of your first contacts should be your family physician and an elder-law attorney who specializes in the legal issues related to aging. Both your family physician and a good elder-law attorney should be able to put you in contact with the professionals and/or communities you might need, such as local assisted living or nursing home facilities.

Some of these professionals will even facilitate with such things as helping your loved one pack and move out of his home, arranging for volunteers to visit or providing a service such as Meals on Wheels. The network of resources will vary depending on your location. If your loved one is still managing fairly well, you may only need visits from a home health aide. If he or she is having more problems with the daily activities of living, but doesn't want – or is not ready – to consider moving into a care facility, you might want to contact an in-home nursing agency.

Try to find professionals who have specific training in understanding the aging process, especially as related to Alzheimer's disease. The more the professional understands the disease, the more she can help with the specific difficulties you and your loved one will encounter. A health care provider will be better able to communicate with and help an individual who has moderate cognitive impairment if she understands the disease, rather than assuming that your loved one simply "doesn't try hard." Ask questions about the professional's experience in caring for older adults. Most importantly, ask yourself this all important question: Would you allow this person to care for your child if you were not there to supervise? Yes, I said "your child." I don't intend to be disrespectful or demeaning. I am merely suggesting that you're considering leaving a loved one, who may be helpless in some ways, in this person's care – and often, particularly when our loved ones still have some degree of cognitive functioning, it's easier to think of your aging relative as a hypothetical child.

If it is at all possible, resist the temptation to ask, "What would I want done for me if I were in this situation?" The healthier and more important question is "what is best for my loved one?" Each individual has different criteria as to what is most important for him and his loved one. Also, don't try to get the professional to give you the answer you want. Have her give you the answer that she feels is best, and then see if you're able to make it work within your goals, beliefs and framework of caring for your loved one.

It helps, at times, to think outside the box. Even when our loved ones require more care and services, for example, we may be able to increase the level of support, structure and supervision required in the home environment to maximize her level of functioning and quality of life.

I previously referred to Ms. Haroldson, and this may be a good opportunity to review her situation as an example of using the system to maintain the status quo. Ms. Haroldson had no family that we knew of, no support network, and the attorney had been appointed to help ascertain her cognitive functioning, specifically as to whether she would be able to remain in her own home. A diminutive woman in her late 70s, never married and without children, Ms. Haroldson completed grammar school and spent her adult life as a factory worker. She was quite sweet in demeanor, but became easily distraught when the topic of potentially displacing her from her home was raised. The assessment process was not very long, as she performed quite poorly on most tasks. I was able to quickly ascertain that her overall level of cognitive functioning was severely affected by dementia, specifically of the Alzheimer's type.

And yet she had been living on her own. Ms. Haroldson was clean and she wasn't malnourished. How had she functioned? Well, in some ways, her social system had taken care of her. Ms. Haroldson's community had taken over, facilitating her needs. Her neighbors had taken over such regular activities as shopping for her and driving her to appointments. In fact, it was because of the neighbors' involvement that her cognitive decline had become apparent, ultimately leading to court involvement. It was clear that Ms. Haroldson could not function independently. And yet, this was one situation where time was on our side.

Except for the disease that was slowly destroying her brain, Ms. Haroldson was apparently quite healthy. There were no records of her having any acute or long-standing illness, and at the time she was not prescribed any medications. But the mere mention of an assisted living facility threw her into a fit of anxiety and despair. She had lived in her home literally all of her life, having inherited the house from her parents upon their passing. She was cognitively appropriate for assisted living, but this was not the right solution for the person she believed she was.

I discussed with her appointed temporary guardian her situation, and together we agreed on a plan of action. He would accept, if agreed upon by the court, permanent guardianship for Ms. Haroldson. He would work to institute specific fail-safe steps to assure that her needs were being attended, such as setting up a Meals on Wheels-type of food delivery program, monitoring her finances, and having an aide visit several days a week to help with hygiene, grooming, and home care. Finally, he would also monitor her overall level of functioning. He agreed that when he saw that she was declining further, even with these support mechanisms in place, he would have the matter reviewed again, to consider further assistance within her home (not likely given her financial situation), or a more structured environment, such as an assisted living or nursing home facility.

Most importantly, all of this was done with the agreement of this lovely woman, whose only desire was to live out her remaining days in her home. She had no insight as to the difficulties of her situation, or how much work would be required on the part of the system, which would be headed by her guardian, whom she clearly liked and trusted. All she knew was that she wanted to be at home, where she felt comfortable. The system was able to work to her advantage.

In this case, staying at home worked out. It doesn't always. One of the most difficult decisions is whether your loved one should be moved into an alternative living situation, such as an assisted living facility or nursing home. There is often a pejorative view of such environments, both for those who might be placed there and their family members. Just under six percent of older adults are actually placed in chronic long-term nursing homes. However, too many people believe that "every old person ends up in a nursing home to die."

If you are struggling with this decision, first and foremost, gain knowledge. Talk to those who have made the decision to place a loved one in such a facility and find out what steps they took to reach it. The ultimate choices made by others are not important, since they may have different reasons for the outcome. But their process might be useful, raising some questions or points of interest that you may not have considered. Ultimately, remind yourself that your goal is to maximize your loved one's quality of life. Being at home just for the sake of not being in a nursing home is not necessarily in your loved one's best interest.

There is a wonderful woman in one of the nursing homes where I consult who is in her late 70s. She came to the facility approximately seven years ago. At the time I was asked to see her because of concerns as to whether she would adjust to the facility, given her relatively young age. Ms. Crowley is a healthy woman, now ambulatory with the use of a rolling walker, but otherwise without difficulty or significant disability. She has a full white head of hair, and when she approaches you can spot her from a distance, as her smile is quite radiant and her greeting always upbeat.

She chose to come to the facility. Ms. Crowley was young and could easily have continued to function within her home setting. She felt that at the time she was doing well enough that she would want to begin the transition *before* it was "too late." My role in our therapy was not to convince her that the nursing home was right for her. She made the choice. My role was to help make the transition easier, as she was not fully aware of the age disparity between her and most of the other residents. We spoke about her interests, and ways in which she could maximize her functioning within the facility by being more active with other residents and taking on a supportive role for those less able, such as encouraging others to participate in activities or even informally visiting with those who cannot leave their rooms as readily. Because she made the active choice to initiate placement, she was more receptive to alternatives and our formal time was relatively short, as she adjusted quite readily and became very involved within the facility. From that time on, without fail, every time I pass her in the hallway she still calls out to me, her smile and greeting as genuine and uplifting as before.

If you do decide that a new living situation is for the best, do your homework. Get references about local facilities. Check out a few in person. After your initial visit, ask for permission to visit at least one or two more times at unscheduled times. Such facilities and their staff will always be on their best behavior initially. Your goal is to see what the place looks like when they're not expecting you. Are the hallways clean and bright, floors safe for those who use a walker or a wheelchair? Are residents up and about? Is there a persistent unpleasant odor throughout the facility? Ask for permission to speak with staff members. Try to assess the turnover rate of the social workers, nursing staff, and physicians. (Note: nurse's aides unfortunately have a notoriously high turnover rate, so that's less of an indicator.) Ask to speak with other family members about their experiences with loved ones living there. Poke about. See if you can have a meal in the dining room. Essentially, you want to take the facility for a test drive. Every facility will look good on paper. Your goal is to ask enough questions and look around enough to convince you and your loved one that he will be reasonably safe and happy there.

The key here, as I've said before, is "reasonable." Throughout the process, we tend to look for certainties and guarantees, and too often there aren't any. In order to get yourself and your loved one through this process, keep the word "reasonable" in mind. You should work to gain reasonable knowledge and put forth reasonable effort. This is key in reducing or eliminating guilt while making monumental decisions.

Caring for Yourself:

As you move ahead with these preparations for your loved one, you cannot forget about yourself – about caring for the caregiver. Sometimes, it helps to simply reach out. If you do, you will quickly realize that you're not alone and that many around you have dealt or are dealing with all the issues you're now facing. I've termed Alzheimer's disease the disease of "one degree of separation." If you talk about it, the person with whom you speak will either have a person suffering with the disease in his family, or know someone who has the disease. Once you're able to acknowledge that you're in need of help, the resource vault will open quickly and broadly.

This is a time when you'll need these resources and you'll benefit from support. This can be a devastating time for the family and loved ones. After years of being with your loved one, mother or father, spouse, brother or sister, you have naturally come to identify them a certain way, to expect them to act in specific ways and fulfill certain roles. That life, those roles, have, or are about to change.

It may help to identify what you're going through as a form of grieving. Even though your loved one is still alive, you're suffering a loss – and anticipating the loss to come. Therefore, it can be helpful to keep in mind the Kubler-Ross stages of grief, as previously discussed in greater depth.

To review, as with any great loss, the first reaction is often one of denial. That's the "everything is fine" phase. The "it must have been the hospital" or the "everyone forgets things" phase. By the time our loved ones have slipped into mid-stage Alzheimer's, many of us have moved past this phase and into anger: "How could this happen to *my* mother. Anyone else, sure, but not *my* mother. There is just no justice in the world."

In Kubler-Ross's classic model, often this is followed by "bargaining." We make deals with God or with fate. We promise to work harder, to devote more time to our ailing parents, to spend all of our money on the best care. This comes from a very natural desire to assert control. It is terrifying to see our lives, our loved ones, taken away from us and to see how random the world – and illness – are. Therefore, we try to pretend that we have some control by offering to sacrifice ourselves. Of course, this doesn't work – and it can exhaust us, our families, and our resources (remember "reasonably"). This can often be followed by depression before reaching the final, desired stage: acceptance.

Of course, we are all individuals. And many of us will find ourselves going back and forth between reactions. After our first angry reactions, for example, many of us tend to cycle back into denial. As soon as we begin taking the first steps toward helping, we tend to shrug off those angry feelings and become falsely optimistic, seeking any possible hope that this is either not true, or will somehow "work out for Mom," regardless of the evidence or what we have seen others go through. We offer comfort, as this gives us comfort. We dismiss our loved one's fears and offer strength and reassurance, as it gives us reassurance (momentary and generally superficial). It is usually when the progression of the disease begins to escalate and becomes more observable that the paths diverge. We have different coping styles. Generally, either we continue to push forward and focus on what "needs to be done", rather than the experience of being with and facilitating our loved one's needs, or we step back and begin to experience the loss in a more real and genuine way.

This is all natural, the process of grief – though, in this case, we experience ***grieving for the living***. Once we begin to see our loved one's decline as it truly is, we actually are able to gain a sense of acceptance. Our sadness, anger, frustration fade into a calm resignation and a letting go, and with that comes a sense of strength and resurrection. Once we have been able to grieve for the person we lost, the intellect and personality that is being stolen by the illness, then we can begin to see the real person in front of us. We can begin to see the loved one who is left, affected by the disease but still human, more accurately, and we can find within ourselves the strength to provide care in the healthiest way – for her, and for us.

Esther is a wonderful example of someone who was able to shift her view of her husband and his decline, so that she could care for him appropriately and in a healthy fashion. When we discussed his disease and the impact it had on his physical and psychological dysfunction, we spoke about the importance of recognizing that, over time, her husband would become almost literally "a shell of his former self." He would look mostly as he did, and maybe even speak with words that sounded familiar. But ultimately, the essence of who he was would be lost to the disease. What would be left was her love and respect for him. In this, she would care for him on his level, but foster and maintain his integrity to his death. When he finally passed away, her sense of loss was not muted. Instead, her grief was a natural progression of a process that had begun some time in the past, when she first took the steps to acknowledge and accept that his cognitive decline would lead to a loss of his identity, leaving her to care for the body, in the form of his illness, but sustain his soul. She mourned each loss as it came, but she cherished the memory of the man her husband had been, and they both benefited from her clear-eyed ability to accept that he was no longer the same.

We must accept that change; we must let ourselves mourn. If we insist that Mom or Dad are still the same as they were, if we continue to rage over that which we cannot control, then we will forever struggle to let go of our anger, resentment, and sadness about their loss. Herman still talks about his wife as she was prior to the disease. He no longer reflects on her last years, when she was significantly impaired by the disease. He reflects on the healthy memory of who she truly was, and as such, she continues to be a healthy force in his life, and the life of her family. By recognizing the disease as something that happens to the body, we are able to shift our focus. What we have then are not memories of the ugly aspects of the disease, but the beauty left by the remembrance of the essence of our loved one.

CHAPTER 7.

Looking Ahead

In recent months, much of my conversation with my family has revolved around long-term planning for my mother. It is time; her cognitive functioning is declining. The decline is, as always, erratic and heartbreaking.

A few months ago, I spoke with her about a very significant personal loss for me and my immediate family. She reacted immediately, with empathy and genuine feeling. "I wish there was something I could do," she said, her face showing that she understood what had happened, even more, perhaps, than I had told her. "I am so sorry."

I could not hold back my tears. I truly felt that I was telling this to my mother. Not a stranger, the woman with Alzheimer's disease that I have been seeing more and more. But by the weekend, when my wife and I met with my parents for dinner, she was gone. The woman who has assumed my mother's form spoke as if she had never heard of my loss. My father seemed irritated with her, as if she were doing it willfully. I briefly closed my eyes. To "explain" to her would not have been helpful, and just then I couldn't explain to my father, yet again, what was happening to her. At that moment, I accepted that there was no reason to tell her again. She would not remember. This was yet another indication of how much further the disease has progressed. It was not too early to plan for the end.

So what are we facing? What, exactly, are our options? Should my mother stay at home, or move to a care facility? If she stays at home, what level of care would she need? If she moves to a facility, then, again, where? What level? And when? When a person is first diagnosed with Alzheimer's, the most natural reaction for the person and caregiver is "whatever you do, don't let me end up in a nursing home". These days the reaction, to some extent, extends to an assisted living facility, though the latter still has a lesser stigma. At the initial stages, the individual and care providers are actively in denial, struggling with acceptance, and as such, planning for the future is almost nonexistent. And yet, we know, with certainty, that the disease is progressive, and generally follows a particular pattern. As such, it would make sense that part of the caregiver process should be to educate and inform individuals about what may be the most difficult part of the caregiving process, considering strategies for the latter stages of the disease.

From a time frame perspective, assuming that the individual struggling with the disease does not have significant concomitant disease processes (e.g. significant heart problems, diabetes), we might expect that the late stage of the disease may occur at about eight years into the process. This obviously will vary based on the specific circumstances of the individual, including the resources available at the beginning of the disease, level of education and functional status prior to the disease onset, as well as ongoing interventions designed to slow the disease process.

Some decisions immediately become clear. My mother could not reasonably live with my family. Our home is not designed to allow her privacy, her increasingly withdrawn behavior would be unhealthy for our children, and neither I nor my wife are in a position to care for her as she declines, both in terms of her physical needs, as well as our work obligations. Nor, do I think, would she willingly accept a home health aide. She is proud, and fancies herself self-sufficient (though she is significantly less so now). She is also very defined in her opinion against having a stranger, an outsider, an employee, helping her with the most intimate of care issues, from hygiene to feeding or more. In addition, home health aides can be extremely expensive, and their services are generally not covered by insurance, though some long-term care insurance does provide some coverage.

One of the first issues we, as caregivers and family members, have to face at this point relates to finances. Sadly, in this society, money defines many of our options. Knowing what we have, what our loved one has, helps us plan realistically.

Because of this, one of the earliest recommendations for loved ones and care providers is to consult with an elder-law attorney and financial advisor. As many older adults will tell you, one of their greatest frustrations, nay, fear, is "losing" their money in old age, mostly due to the concerns of not having enough to afford long-term care if needed and having to be subsidized by public assistance (namely Medicaid), being dependent on family members, not having sufficient resources to leave to a surviving spouse, and not being able to pass on money to their children and grandchildren. These days, elder-law attorneys and financial advisors will tell you that it is never too early to consider long-term care insurance. In my mother's case, she started too late and it was no longer an option.

Generally speaking, an elder-care lawyer's primary concern is to protect the person's financial resources. As long-term care can be extremely expensive and may easily deplete someone's assets, one goal is to protect the assets from the potential need to "spend down" that is required before a person becomes eligible for Medicaid assistance. This "spend down," as many care providers and family members already know, basically requires individuals to have exhausted their own resources before state or federal assistance kicks in. The matter may be further complicated if the loved one for whom you are caring has a spouse and finances are held jointly. The "spend down" may potentially leave the spouse with very limited resources. Depending on your loved one's income, you might benefit from discussing in advance ways of investing her money appropriately, so that he or she might be able to generate income as well as protect it in the event of the need for extended care.

When considering financial issues, the financial demands for taking care of a loved one with Alzheimer's disease can be significant, as home health care workers, assisted living, or nursing home care can be very expensive. Home health aide workers can range in cost, but at least as of today, are, at times, only marginally different in overall cost from an assisted living facility, assuming that your loved one requires full time care. To the extent that only a few hours are required, clearly from a financial perspective, a health care worker is preferable, costing in the range of $12 to $20 an hour.

Assuming that there are medical complications or limitations which require a more intensive level of care, your loved one may not only benefit from, but may require an assisted living or nursing home facility, depending on her strengths and limitations. It's important to clarify that having Alzheimer's disease is not, in and of itself, a reason for placing a loved one in an assisted living or nursing home facility. It is when concomitant factors, namely behavioral and medical concerns, arise, that a more structured environment becomes a consideration or necessity.

The first level of care out side of the home can often be found in what is now commonly called "assisted living." Assisted living facilities have become ubiquitous in recent years, and have increased in size and services. Generically speaking, these involve renting an "apartment" in a facility, which comes with a range of services, such as meals and housekeeping and the services of personal aides. However, they do require that their resident have some mobility and at least limited functioning (this is, after all, "assisted" living, not completely facilitated living). Depending on the locale and range of services offered, a good assisted living facility can cost from as little as a couple of thousand dollars a month to more than five thousand dollars monthly.

It seems useful to take a moment here and reflect on an increasingly popular option: the continuing care retirement community (also known as CCRC). These increasingly popular options are presented more as "communities for active seniors," and while an increasing number have assisted living and nursing home, or even dedicated Alzheimer's wings, they may require applicants to enter while still functioning at a very high, independent level. In addition, they can be pricey. Most of these facilities require that your loved one "buy into" the apartment, basically, purchase a condo in the development, as well as pay monthly fees. However, for people who still retain a high level of functioning and yet want to prepare for a potential decline, this may be an option.

Within both assisted living and CCRC facilities, additional daily costs may be incurred for other services, including cleaning, providing meals in the room, bathing and grooming, and medication management.

Nursing homes are the next option, and are really for those who no longer can function independently, and may need a range of assistance, such as assistance with meals, mobility, and attending activities. With a much greater degree of care provided, nursing home costs have increased dramatically in the past few years, now ranging from four to seven thousand dollars a month. However, for these much higher fees, nursing homes provide virtually around-the-clock care, from feeding to personal hygiene, as necessary. Obviously, this is a choice for those whose loved ones really require this level of care. The primary consideration for placement in a nursing home should be whether your loved one requires the level of care that you, an assisted living facility, or home health worker are unable to provide, and in receiving this level of care, will maximize your loved one's quality of life.

As for my parents, while they are both with us – particularly as long as my father is able and willing to be the primary caregiver for my mother – we seem to have more options. Therefore, it's appropriate to explore options for both of my parents. I spoke with my parents about sharing a home with an in-law apartment. They were receptive. I was somewhat surprised by this, because for all that they rely upon me, they still retain a strong sense of independence. But they were amenable, and together we started looking into a home with an in-law suite. This kind of situation might not work if we lost my father, but for now – for the immediate future – it might be the easiest option. The one that would change everyone's lives in the least disruptive way.

Except that it wasn't possible. After considerable searching, we found that in our area such housing is scarce. Nor is building an addition onto our existing home possible. The first option, one that might have been a stop-gap at best, has been eliminated.

My wife recently suggested that I consider looking into nursing home facilities in Israel. She based this on the idea that my mother might feel more comfortable in an environment familiar to her from her younger years. Though my mother has been fluent in English, she's now losing her command of this language. The decline of her Hebrew, her primary language, seems to be slower. The financial cost of such a facility in Israel is not significantly less, and there's no guarantee that this familiarity would necessarily benefit my mother. My father is not inclined to return to Israel, and my mother would have no one to regularly visit her. Though both of my parents have siblings in Israel, they, too, are aging and would not be able to oversee my mother's care. If my mother were to remain here, at least I could oversee her care in a local facility, possibly even facilitate placing her in a facility where I am a consultant, and my father and our family could visit frequently.

Interestingly enough, when my mother was previously hospitalized for medical concerns, her attending physician suggested having her placed in a nursing home for rehabilitation, mostly to give my father a break. I readily agreed and started making the initial contacts necessary to facilitate the process. My planning, as has been the case in many a situation with my parents, was premature. My father's ongoing struggle to understand and accept the distinction between my mother's prior personality style and her present disease process interfered with his ability to recognize the value of such temporary placement, a term commonly referred to as "respite," designed to help both the individual as well as care provider shore up strengths. When I spoke to him about this, he readily agreed it would help him regain some of his equanimity and strength, while allowing the facility to help my mother strengthen physically, and give her "round the clock" care, something she would clearly "enjoy."

Short-term respite and other kinds of facility stays have become much more common, wide ranging, and accepted. These vary greatly. Rehabilitation stays have become quite common in recent years. Often times, following hospital stays, individuals require physical rehabilitation, to regain strength as well as master previously routine rudimentary tasks, now lost through disuse. Most "rehab" stays, however, are temporary, pending a move back to independent living or some kind of nursing care, either a long-term nursing home or assisted living facility. These are quite separate options. Whereas in the past placement in an assisted living facility was considered simply a transition to long-term nursing home care, now it's regarded as a different kind of service, one which allows the individual to extend his or her level of independence in the community. In my mother's case, the cost would have been covered by health insurance, in this case Medicare and supplemental insurance.

And yet, when the attending physician at the hospital approached my mother about this topic, she balked and stated she didn't need nursing care, likely because she was not clear as to the full extent and value of this short term placement. To her rescue, my father quickly chimed in saying such a stay was unnecessary. Despite our earlier discussions in which he had agreed that he could have used the break, now he was adamant. He was perfectly able to take care of my mother and bring her home. For him, her potential unhappiness superseded his need for respite. This highlights the notion that "the best laid plans" are sometimes frustrated.

If the timeline of the disease holds consistent, my mother may have another three to five years. Three to five years in which the disease will further debilitate her. As such, the level of care she will need will become much greater than at present, a level that my father is not capable of providing.

As I read what I just wrote, I realize that it sounds like I'm anticipating the worst. I am. In my professional role I have seen what this disease does to people. I have witnessed the later stages, and expect that, barring acute terminal illness, my mother will progressively decline and move into the final stage of the disease. This may be an appropriate point to describe in greater detail what I expect for my mother's future, because likely this is what other readers may experience with their loved ones.

At the mid-stage of the disease, functional abilities are still somewhat intact, though fraying. Functional independence is challenged, but not yet taken away completely. Verbal communication still seems to be intact, though closer scrutiny reveals some gaps, such as difficulty in maintaining fluent conversation and the "forgetting" of commonly used words. Activities of daily living may be managed, but not with ease, and if left to their own devices, difficulties will become apparent, such as mismanagement of finances, inconsistent medication regimen, and even emotionally, in the form of irritability or depression.

As the person transitions to the latter stage of the disease, functional abilities decline further. Even if the person doesn't want assistance, it becomes clear that he needs it to fulfill basic daily activities. He will no longer effectively manage self hygiene and grooming, and will require assistance not only in preparing of meals, but possibly even in eating. At this stage, the neurons in the brain, responsible for sending messages to the body, have died at a significant rate, and continue to do so with every passing day. It is at this point that maximizing independence and integrity requires that we do for our loved one, rather than assuming that he can still function independently.

This may be the most difficult process yet for caregivers, as they watch their loved ones become physically, cognitively and psychologically unable to function. Experiences differ. Some people become clearly physically frail, and there is no doubt of their inability. Others may not physically decline in an obvious way, and the struggle for the caregiver is to recognize that despite physically appearing to be able, the loved one is cognitively infirm and thereby requires help just as if he were physically infirm.

Herman experienced this type of decline at the latter stages of his wife's disease. His wife suffered a rare form of the disease, one which afflicts less than 10 percent of those suffering with Alzheimer's disease, in which the disease occurs prior to the age of 65, often with a shorter life span and an acute time frame for physical and cognitive decline. Ruth had been in the nursing home only slightly longer than a year when she began to decline more rapidly. Before that she had held her own at home, with the help of her husband and primarily one of her sons.

Herman was always very active in trying to secure his wife's well-being, even at the nursing home. He visited regularly and was always assured that she was receiving the care that he believed she needed. However, he often found it difficult to believe that the decline he witnessed was in fact due to the disease, rather than a lack of staff involvement. He was steadfast in his belief that Ruth should continue to receive what is commonly referred to as restorative care, helping her walk daily to keep her body in motion. As the disease was taking over, Ruth was no longer able to walk, even with assistance. Herman struggled with this, believing that if the staff made the attempt, she would succeed. In our conversations, we focused on the difference between willingness and ability, and the notion that, regardless of the staff's willingness and participation, his wife's abilities were declining, and neither the staff nor he could "will" them back.

Eventually, even Ruth's wishes were lost. Ruth's disease had progressed such that she was no longer able to meaningfully communicate. Her speech was so impaired as to be what is known as "word salad," a presentation where the person uses words that, without context, have clear meaning, but that within the sentence make absolutely no sense: "I dog and whoever why I so and Sue..."

For the individual at the end stage of the disease who is still able to communicate, it is important to focus on what she can do, rather than what you wish she could do. The intent is not to discourage your loved one, if she is able to express a desire, rather to maintain the highest level of functioning and quality of life possible. When the possibility is not there, not due to her unwillingness but rather due to inability, allowing her to "try" will only exacerbate a sense of failure. The neurons have died, and will not regenerate. The messages from the brain to the body that say "walk" are not working. Encouraging or facilitating her desire to walk, "willing" the legs to walk, may foster a greater sense of despair and loss, than focusing on what she is still able to do.

Rather than fighting the decline, it's important to shore up your loved one's resources. At no stage am I suggesting to give up and do nothing. Instead, the goal is to shift the focus of your efforts from trying to help your loved one do for herself, to make sure she receives optimal level of care to sustain her integrity and well being. The most unfortunate, and unbalanced, image we have of older adults are those in the nursing home, huddled in the wheelchair, drooling, babbling, or inextricably calling out. At the end-stages of the disease, there is no doubt that the disease will win out physically and cognitively, but we have the ability, as caregivers, to help our loved ones sustain their integrity.

Rather than forcing staff to have Ruth continue to walk, we worked to help Herman accept that caring for her in bed was in her best interest, reducing her physical and emotional distress. Instead of insisting that she eat independently, feeding her allowed Herman and Ruth yet another moment where they could connect, working through the opportunity so that Herman could say his goodbyes in a warm and giving way, rather than in an angry and resentful manner.

And so, I return back to considering possible choices available for my mother, and what course might be expected as the disease progresses. For me, as for many family members, this is a difficult undertaking.

When my mother was healthy, she had no interest in such a discussion, and did not believe it applied to her. I don't suppose that her responses would be much different now than they had been in the past. We don't talk about it so as not to foster a sense of despair, or even anger, "are you planning for my demise already?" My father remains of this similar view regarding himself to this day. Once he participated in the process of the living will, it's as if he completely put it out of his mind. Beyond that brief process, I have never been able to engage him in the most benign conversation about what he would like done if he were to become incapacitated due to a stroke or other catastrophic illness. His generic and persistent response has been "don't worry, I'm not going anywhere, and when I do, it'll be quick." He struggles to understand that death is not the same thing as incapacity, and that, on some level, incapacity can be worse than a quick death.

My mother, in casual conversations, has volunteered generic statements, saying in an offhand manner that she'd want us to "pull the plug" or "I wouldn't want to live like that." I believe these reflect her deeper wishes. My mother would not enjoy a prolonged experience of physical disability. Presently, her life is quite limited qualitatively and my goal is to maximize her quality of life.

Caregivers are understandably reluctant to initiate such discussions. They make us feel morbid, as if we were the Grim Reaper, standing in wait with a dastardly grin. Ultimately, in taking on the role of caregiver, we must look inside ourselves and recognize that our motivation is pure and genuine. Once we are able to do so, the conversations will flow, and the choices will be made. They will not be good or bad, right or wrong. They will be healthy.

People approach discussions and decision-making in their own way. For my parents, the situation was made somewhat easier by my ability to recognize the need to seek support outside my area of specialty. In creating their living wills, my parents met with an attorney who gently, yet with great detail, went through a decision making process with them. Her role was not just that of a counselor, but rather an educator and support system. She explained to them what they might encounter, discussed the implications, and allowed them to make the choices best suited for them.

Some people prefer a list, not unlike the one presented by an elder-law attorney helping in the process of preparing a living will: "What would you want done if you could not talk? What if you were in a coma?" Other people may be more comfortable with a fluid conversation, in which ideas are discussed, without necessarily making choices in the moment: "I believe that once the brain stops working, there is really no point to sustaining life." "I think if I stopped eating, it probably would signal that I was ready to go." Some caregivers rehearse their conversation, or have incremental conversations, where they broach the topics in small steps. Whichever style you and your loved one find comfortable, make sure that these conversations continue until you have a strong sense that you understand your loved one's intentions and desires. If they can be set forth in a written living will, that will hopefully avoid any confusion if and when the need should arise. These decisions are usually not simple, but having a good sense of your loved one's desires can minimize the anxiety and potential guilt.

These conversations are difficult, no doubt about it. But try to recognize that, in your role of caregiver, you are being entrusted to preserve your loved one's integrity and beliefs. Don't shy away from gaining knowledge about the issues that will likely need to be addressed in the future. Don't assume that mom will live in a vegetative state for years. Ask her what her thoughts are about living under such circumstances, and what she thinks would be in her best interest. Don't avoid direct questions: "What if you were no longer able to feed yourself? Would you accept a feeding tube? What if you were physically infirm and required total care? If there was no money available for in-home care, how would you feel about a nursing home placement?"

Of course, you may run into difficulties. If, for example, your mother says "no matter what, never put me in a nursing home," you have a dilemma. Try to talk about the options: assisted living, for example, offers independence, but with help. Try to encourage your loved one to be open about such realistic possibilities, especially if you, as the caregiver, have other significant responsibilities or are limited financially. Try to work with your loved one on contingencies and flexibility, to address various possible scenarios with a variety of options while still honoring her belief system at its core.

The hope is that your loved one understands and is willing to work with the limitations of his situation as well as yours. Sometimes that's not the case. I have a client who was placed in a nursing home approximately a year and half ago by his children. His wife was placed there some time before him. He was (and remains) physically well, relatively speaking. At the time he was moved to the facility, he struggled with his placement there. I was asked to see him, and in my evaluation, I noted that his ability to encode and retain new information was limited, and I believed that this hindered his ability to "accept" placement. Every session was essentially the same conversation, "my kids have money. They should take us home." After some effort, I discontinued treatment due to his inability to consider alternatives. Recently I was asked to re-visit with him for the exact same reason. I did, and his presentation was identical to what I had seen over a year ago. The same complaints; the same belief that his children had sufficient money and should care for him and his wife. I again made numerous efforts to help him understand that the issue was not his children's financial abilities, but rather that they did not have the overall resources to care for his wife and him. Ironically, it was his wife who confronted me after a session, stating that all I was doing was making her husband feel bad.

"Stop telling him things like that," she said. In essence, their perception was such that, no matter what anyone said, and no matter how anyone tried to frame the situation, they would not accept the value and need for placement.

Could this situation have been avoided? At this point, it seems irredeemable. In an ideal world, the hope is that these issues can be addressed early on, when minds are clear and unencumbered by the intensity of the issues surrounding the disease. However, the basic choices remain, even if your loved one is inflexible. He or she may chose someone else who may fulfill her wishes in absolute terms, but, if no one else is available, or able, than you must, in good conscious, do what you believe is best, under the circumstances, recognizing that your role is not to harm yourself in caring for your loved one. That doesn't benefit anyone.

Again, recognize that your efforts are laudable and that you are motivated by your loved one's best interest. Just because your parents' next door neighbor or best friend died in his bed, doesn't mean you need to avoid the possibility that your parent, struggling with end-stage Alzheimer's disease, may require a nursing home placement. Waiting until it's too late will actually foster a greater sense of guilt and distress for you, and possibly for your loved one. Don't assume that mom will go into an assisted living facility or nursing home, but strengthen your support network by looking into the possibility and identifying some feasible options in advance. Don't assume that her finances will need to be depleted because she will require 24-hour care, but certainly talk to an elder-law attorney about how to best preserve her assets for the long run. Consider worst-case scenarios. For example, what if you agree to provide your father with a home health aide, and he runs each one that comes in the door out in under a day? What if you mother willingly enters an assisted living facility, only to turn around and express a sense of regret and calls you every day complaining and asking to leave, after her home has already been sold? These are issues that may occur, and are not unreasonable to consider in advance. Discussing and considering their implications does not make you an ogre, it makes you better able to reasonably protect and preserve your loved one's wishes and integrity, if and when the time comes.

Finally, you will need to question even the premise that you will be able to be there, to help and actively participate in caring for your loved one though her passing. My assumption is that even if my father passes away before my mother, I will still be available for her. I do not assume I will die in the next five years, but what if circumstances change in such a way that I am not able to care for my mother? What if I am disabled by an accident or become ill, or have other demands in my immediate family? We must always make contingencies for the unlikely.

In my case, I have a truly selfless second line of care. My wife has agreed to step into my role of secondary care provider. She has been actively involved to date: talking with and listening to my mother as our discussions about finances, physical and cognitive infirmity, and even burial plots have occurred. One of the wonderful things about my wife's participation is her desire to better understand my mother's process of decline, and to understand why my father struggles as he does in understanding her disease. In doing so, she becomes a more effective surrogate for me, as the secondary care provider, if I could not fulfill this role, and primary if something were to happen to my father. At the very least, she is a wonderful support to me as I facilitate my mother's care now and for the future.

Closing Thoughts:

As part of my work, I travel the country educating professionals and lay people about Alzheimer's disease and other dementias. These talks are long and involved; I commonly speak for six hours, with only a break for lunch. Over the years, I have learned several important things during these seminars – both about my audiences and myself. Even when I speak to professionals, I have found, it is clear that they are there not only because of their professional role, but because they have, or maybe anticipate, a personal connection For myself, I have discovered that although I have been a seminar presenter for several years, I have never once felt tired or bored.

I have a passion for working with older adults. I know it comes from my experiences growing up with my grandparents. It's an absolutely accurate statement that in my work, I have never met an older adult I didn't like, regardless of the concerns that brought us together, be it a psychological issue such as depression, or behavioral difficulties related to dementia. I feel a genuine connection, a bond, in listening to an older adult tell his story, and helping him focus on ways he can feel significant in his life.

That doesn't change when I meet a person with Alzheimer's disease, regardless of the stage of the disease. My goal in writing this book is to help care providers view their loved ones in a more realistic way, but also in a more genuine way. The disease has a global impact, both for the individual who suffers with Alzheimer's and those around him. In better understanding the disease and its implications, cognitively, psychologically, behaviorally, we become better able to care *for* those whom we care *about.*

At my seminars, I conclude with a story of a time when I was speaking at a hotel facility that was also hosting another affair in an adjoining conference hall. The event was for older adult volunteers from a local hospital. During one of my breaks I strolled around and observed what could only be described as unbridled frivolity. Over 200 older adults, singing and dancing, celebrating the time of their life. It was genuinely heartening to watch them, not because of their age (you know, even older adults can have fun), but because they truly represent the older adult population. Vibrant, energized. The purpose of the story is to remind the participants at my seminar that while we tend to focus on Alzheimer's disease during the session, which creates a disproportionately negative view of older adults, we need to remember that most older adults are the ones who attended that celebration, and further, that even with the disease, older adults should not stop *truly* living.

For those of us who are preparing for, or already care for an older adult loved one, it is important to maintain a sense of balance and perspective for ourselves as well as the person for whom we are caring. Sir Francis Bacon is attributed as having said "for also knowledge itself is power," colloquially recalled simply as "knowledge is power." The more information we gain about the disease, the better we are able to help our struggling loved one, as well as ourselves. But it is important to keep things in perspective and not let ourselves be overwhelmed by our desire to know, in essence "to control" the outcome of the disease. See your loved one as he is, and this will free you to be who you are. You need not become a superhero.

Gain reasonable knowledge and put forth reasonable effort.

Finally, with all the information we have about Alzheimer's disease, its behavioral manifestations and impact on the brain, we can never be certain of what else may or may not be going on inside the person struggling with the disease. As such, while we imperatively must shift our view of our loved one, and behave in ways that at times may seem as if we are infantilizing him, we must always remind ourselves that at the core is a person, someone who deserves our respect, compassion, and care. Some people assume that when the disease reaches its end stage, the person struggling with the disease has no awareness or ability to meaningfully process any information, thoughts, or feelings. Others will suggest that certain experiences transcend our understanding, our knowledge of how the human being "works." I suggest that in gaining knowledge about Alzheimer's disease, its impact on our loved one and ourselves, we keep tucked away, a bit of hope, reasonable or otherwise.

The disease is external. The soul is eternal.

For Further Information...

If you have questions for Dr. Steinberg, would like more information about Dr. Steinberg's work or an opportunity to attend one of his nationwide seminars, please log on to www.caregivingforcaregivers. com. This site will also allow you or a loved one to take a brief cognitive assessment, which will be interpreted directly by Dr. Steinberg. You may also e-mail Dr. Steinberg with any comments or if you would like additional resources.

Made in the USA
Middletown, DE
19 December 2019